GLASGOW TRAM

A PICTORIAL TRIBUT

MARKING THE 60TH ANNIVERSAR
OF THE CLOSURE IN 1962

Front c
vehicle
Tony Bel

Half tit
an ever
busy he
How ap

Back cov
here at

Back cov
'Coronat

Back cov
Trams w

Ticket 1 (green)

1894 – 1962

Cunarder 1379 - The Last.

FAREWELL TO GLASGOW'S TRAMS
1894 – 1962

Last Tram Procession Souvenir Ticket

DALMARNOCK ROAD to POLLOKSHAWS ROAD
4th SEPTEMBER, 1962

1894 – 1962

Ticket 2 (green)

A		0319
Dalmarnock Road	**2'6**	Bridgeton Cross
Bridgeton Cross		Kent Street
Kent Street		Queen Street
Queen Street		Argyle Street
Argyle Street		Cook Street
Cook Street		Eglinton Toll
Eglinton Toll		Pollokshaws Road

GLASGOW CORPORATION TRANSPORT
Issued subject to Bye-laws. Ticket available only on Tram on which it was issued. NOT TRANSFERABLE.

Glasgow Numerical Ptg. Co. Ltd.

Ticket 3 (orange)

1894 – 1962

FAREWELL TO GLASGOW'S TRAMS
1894 – 1962

LAST TRAM SOUVENIR TICKET

ANDERSTON CROSS and AUCHENSHUGGLE
2nd, 3rd and 4th SEPTEMBER, 1962

1894 – 1962

Ticket 4 (orange)

1174. AN x 5

C		7147
Auchenshuggle	**6d**	Maukinfauld Road
Maukinfauld Road		1777 London Road
1277 London Road		Fraser Street
Fraser Street		Bridgeton Cross
Bridgeton Cross		Kent Street
Kent Street		Queen Street
Queen Street		Anderston Cross

GLASGOW CORPORATION TRANSPORT
Issued subject to Bye-laws. Ticket available only on Tram on which it was issued. NOT TRANSFERABLE.

Glasgow Numerical Ptg. Co. Ltd.

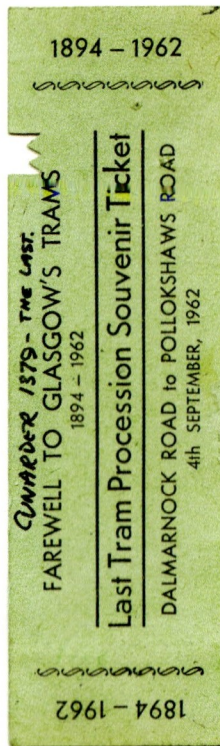

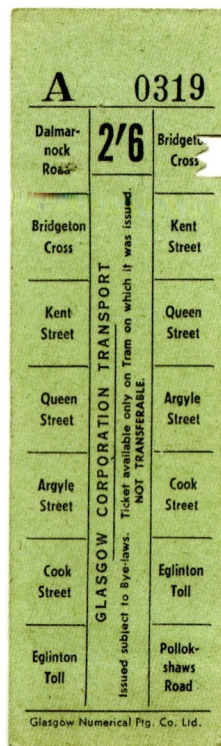

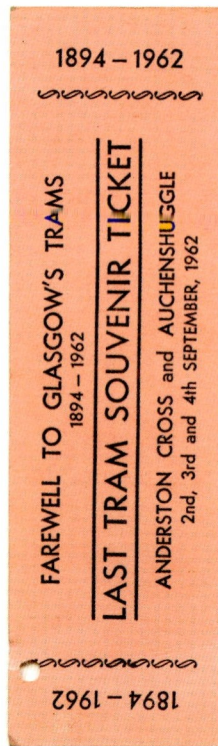

ver: An estimated 250,000 people witnessed the passing of the 'caurs' on 4 September 1962 when a parade of 20 trams, including a number of magnificently restored made their final journeys through the wet city streets. Nothing, however, could dampen people's affection for a mode of transport which had served them so well.

page: Lines of trams in the street are usually depicting breakdowns, power cuts or something outside the ordinary. Much rarer is someone taking the trouble to record lay scene like this. Here for all to see is what Glasgow trams were all about. A rolling double deck conveyor belt, transporting citizens effortlessly up Renfield Street in the t of the city without producing any pollution. Imagine if everyone had used a bus or car. The film showing at the Odeon *They Rode West* dates this lost world as 1954. ropriate if the film had carried the title *They Rode West, East and North by Tram*! *Bob Docherty collection/Online Transport Archive*

er (top left): The trams not only served busy city streets but, in places, they also penetrated into the surrounding countryside, sometimes on their own private tracks as biersbridge. *E.C. Bennett & Martin Jenkins/Online Transport Archive*

er (top right): Among the hundreds of new trams built by the Corporation at their extensive Coplawhill works were the famous and much-admired double-decker on' and 'Cunarder' type cars which during the final years dominated the dwindling number of heavily-used services. *Tony Belton*

er (bottom): Services along the Dumbarton Road corridor along the north bank of the Clyde crossed the Forth & Clyde Canal by means of a swing bridge at Dalmuir. re sometimes delayed by the passage of waterway vessels. *David F. Russell*

GLASGOW TRAMS
A PICTORIAL TRIBUTE

MARKING THE 60TH ANNIVERSARY
OF THE CLOSURE IN 1962

MARTIN JENKINS AND GEOFF PRICE

PEN & SWORD
TRANSPORT

AN IMPRINT OF PEN & SWORD BOOKS LTD.
YORKSHIRE ~ PHILADELPHIA

First published in Great Britain in 2022 by
Pen and Sword Transport
An imprint of
Pen & Sword Books Ltd.
Yorkshire - Philadelphia

Typeset by SJmagic DESIGN SERVICES, India.
Printed and bound in India by Replika Press Pvt. Ltd.

Pen & Sword Books Ltd incorporates the Imprints of Pen & Sword Books Archaeology, Atlas, Aviation, Battleground, Discovery, Family History, History, Maritime, Military, Naval, Politics, Railways, Select, Transport, True Crime, Fiction, Frontline Books, Leo Cooper, Praetorian Press, Seaforth Publishing, Wharncliffe and White Owl.

For a complete list of Pen & Sword titles please contact

PEN & SWORD BOOKS LIMITED
47 Church Street, Barnsley, South Yorkshire, S70 2AS, England
E-mail: enquiries@pen-and-sword.co.uk
Website: www.pen-and-sword.co.uk

or

PEN AND SWORD BOOKS
1950 Lawrence Rd, Havertown, PA 19083, USA
E-mail: Uspen-and-sword@casematepublishers.com
Website: www.penandswordbooks.com

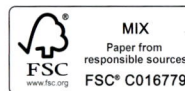

FSC
www.fsc.org
MIX
Paper from
responsible sources
FSC® C016779

INTRODUCTION

There have been several very good photo albums of Glasgow trams plus a number of authoritative books on different aspects of Glasgow's remarkable tram system. To mark the 60th anniversary of the closure, when some 250,000 people lined the streets to watch the final procession, this book takes a different path by following in detail the abandonment programme in chronological order from 1948 to 1962. Our aim is to show as many different aspects and areas of the city as possible, some of which are rarely seen in photographs.

To achieve this, we have assembled a wealth of black and white and colour images, most of them previously unpublished, and we have opted to include as many as possible by showing up to four to a page in order to give people a unique overview of each abandoned service or section. We were partly inspired to take this approach by an article published in *Modern Tramway* in June 1959 in which the distinguished tramway historian John Price wrote:

In years to come, our retrospect pictures of Glasgow's trams will be an empty car standing sadly at a terminus, a robot in a robot setting. They are not like that at all. When we try to remember the details in 10 or 20 years hence (or sixty), we won't get the right idea from films taken entirely in sunlit suburbs. Walk along streets whose architecture has hardly changed in thirty years, junctions with trams on all five

streets, shipyard crowds, the 4.30pm turn out from a depot, the 5.30pm kaleidoscope at Union Street crossing, trams in convoy for ten destinations, the crew change at a depot and the view from an upstairs window of a tram.

We hope in some small way we have followed John's advice and put the trams back where they belong on streets all over the city with people, period buses, cars and lorries, shops, churches, theatres, cinemas, parks, shipyards, factories and even steam locos running on the tram tracks. Furthermore, our coverage goes way beyond the city boundary out as far as Airdrie, Coatbridge, Cambuslang, Rutherglen, Barrhead, Paisley, Renfrew, Clydebank and Milngavie. Over the years, many of our chosen locations have changed beyond recognition whilst others remain instantly recognisable. Our earliest colour views date back to the time when the older trams displayed the city's famous identifying coloured route bands – blue, green, red, yellow or white – on the panels between the upper and lower deck windows. Some of these early colour images have been included for their rarity value. We hope you will enjoy looking back as much as we have.

Martin Jenkins
Walton-on-Thames

Geoff Price
Halton-on-Lune

DEDICATION

This book is dedicated to John Clarke who visited Glasgow as a young man and walked many routes taking photographs along the way, none of which have been published before. It is also dedicated to Hamish Stevenson and to the memory of Brian Longworth, Struan Robertson, Ian Stewart, David Thomson and Richard Wiseman who did so much to record aspects of the Glasgow trams.

During the course of our research, we have drawn on many books, newspaper articles, magazines, leaflets, timetables, personal notes, anecdotes and memories.

ACKNOWLEDGEMENTS

We should like to thank all the photographers who have made their images available; the National Tramway Museum for permission to use Richard Wiseman images; Charles Roberts for technical support; Barry 'Curly' Cross for his generosity; David A. Brown, Bob Docherty, Hamish Stevenson, Richard Sykes and Garth Tilt for help with background information, unearthing photographs and identifying locations; the Scottish Tramway & Transport Society for making their photographic archive available; and Stuart Little for observations and proof reading. Tony Wilson kindly granted access to the W.D. McMillan collection held by Travel Lens Photographic. Tony may be contacted through the Transport Memorabilia Shop, Unit 3, Tramway Close (ex-Whitehouse Close), Laxey, Isle of Man, IM4 7BA, close to the Manx Electric Railway station. (Ring 01624 861898 for opening hours.)

I was first introduced to the magic of Glasgow trams in the summer of 1954. It was love at first sight. Until the system closed in 1962, I made many visits to record the passing of the trams graduating from a basic brownie box camera to colour slides and 8mm and 9.5mm cine film the costs being shared latterly with my great school friend Chris Bennett. Hailing from Merseyside, I always had a soft spot for the ex-Liverpool cars and during 1959/60 as Chairman of the Liverpool University Public Transport Society, and later the Merseyside Tramway Preservation Society, I was closely involved in the purchase for preservation of 1055 (Liverpool 869). I shall never forget the marathon six-hour, fund-raising tour when 1055 left St Vincent Street on 21 February 1960 with 94 passengers on board. Following the closure, I kept in touch with many enthusiasts in Glasgow, some now sadly no longer with us, and each year I would travel to the city to give a slide presentation. Afterwards, hours would vanish as we shared our memories. My lasting regret – that I was unable to see 1282 make its farewell run to and from Clydebank on 6 September 1962. (Martin)

My first visit to Glasgow was in February 1961. Standing on the corner of Union Street and Argyle Street instantly brought back similarities with my home city, Liverpool. Trams moving in convoy along streets of granite setts, enclosed by shops and offices; further out the gaunt tenements, which seem to go on for miles, were in contrast to the wider open spaces of suburban Glasgow. Subsequently, several visits were made to the city in the company of Martin Jenkins and Allan Clayton, travelling through the night by car from Merseyside to reach Glasgow as its citizens were waking up. Riding on 1379 at the rear of the final procession on 4 September was an experience vividly recalled whenever I hear *Telstar* played on the radio or CD – the Tornados No. 1 hit record in the charts on 30 August 1962. For many tram enthusiasts it became synonymous with the end of the trams. In 1999, Stuart Little introduced me to Brian Longworth who revived my interest in Glasgow. His knowledge of the transport department and its workings coupled with his comprehensive collection of GCT material, provided many hours of enjoyment and knowledge for me. The friendship endured up to his untimely death in 2016. (Geoff)

Tribute to the staff of Glasgow Corporation Tramways. *Charles Bilette, David Brown, R.A. Connor, Brian Longworth*, G.W. Price*, Hamish Stevenson*, R.J.S. Wiseman/ National Tramway Museum (*Online Transport Archive)*

GLASGOW CORPORATION TRAMWAYS
1 JANUARY 1948

* Services via Renfield St.
1, 3, 5, 5A, 8, 14, 14A
24, 25, 30 & 32

Based on J C Gillham original, 1958
Drawn by R A Smith, 2001
Adapted for this volume by Charles Roberts

1947

The purpose of this book is to cover the abandonment programme in date order with photographic profiles of each discontinued section or service. By 1947, Glasgow had the largest system in the UK. Despite war-time deprivations, the undertaking was on the road to recovery with the 'caurs' still seen as having a long-term future. The 300 mile network had 11 depots, a self-contained tramcar-building and repair works at Coplawhill, a permanent way yard, a sand drying plant, a driver training school, a Corporation-owned power station and associated substations. Some 1,200 trams were available to cover a peak demand for 973 cars, the majority of which were the durable Round-Dash and Hex-Dash Standards built mainly at Coplawhill between 1898 and 1924 and numbered variously between **1-1088**, with the oldest being **696**. By 1930, the majority had 8ft wheelbase trucks, two 60hp motors, air-wheel and track brakes. Complementing these were a group of cars acquired from Paisley District Tramway in 1923. Numbered variously between **1009-1072**, some had been cut down to single-deckers and some double-deckers reduced in height. **1090-1140** were maximum traction double truck cars delivered from various body-builders during 1927/28 of which one, **1100**, was rebuilt in 1941. Coronation Mark I cars, **1141-1292**, built at Coplawhill between 1937 and 1941 rode on EMB lightweight bogies and had four 35hp motors. Notable one-offs included Standard **142**, lengthened in 1927 as a prototype bogie car, and **1089**, a high-speed experimental single-decker built at Coplawhill in 1926 which had four 25hp motors and rode on equal wheel Brill 77E bogies. Lightweight two-axle cars **6, 1001-1004** were built at Coplawhill between 1940 and 1943 with a mix of trucks and motors. Finally, uni-directional double-decker **1005** of 1947 had inside frame Maley & Taunton trucks, four 45hp motors and Vambac control equipment. Photographs of these types including some of the variations will be seen throughout the book.

The Corporation also maintained an impressive works fleet, most being former passenger cars although some were purpose-built.

1898: No. 3, Dalmarnock depot, 3 January 1943. Seen with war-time white fender, this was an original 'room and kitchen' car of 1898 converted 10 years later into a Mains Department testing vehicle which required four 30hp motors in order to transport heavy rotary converter equipment. After withdrawal in 1953 it was stored for preservation and is now a star exhibit at the Glasgow Museum of Transport. *Martin Jenkins collection/Online Transport Archive*

1900: No. 23, Great Western Road, 1 April 1960. Standard 814 was rebuilt into this Tool Car in 1954. Here it transports gas canisters for track lifting at Knightswood. It was sold in October 1962. *David A. Brown*

1904: No. 20, Argyle Street, 1955. Ex-Paisley 39 was the last unvestibuled tram in the fleet. Powered by two 30hp motors and mounted on a 6ft wheelbase truck, it served as a Mains Department Tool Van from 1925 to 1959. *Phil Tatt/Online Transport Archive*

1904: No. 27, Union Street, September 1959. This ex-Paisley District car became a Tool Van in the 1930s. It was fitted with a vestibule in 1938 and given equipment from a withdrawn 'Regen' car in the 1950s. During September 1959, it was the last works car to be transformed into an illuminated advertising car, in this instance for a Scottish Industries Exhibition. *G.W. Price collection*

1905: No. 1, Ruby Street, Dalmarnock. 1960. Operated by the Mains Department, this cable-laying car with its own trailer carried large cable drums which were unloaded from the rear. It is now preserved. *Struan Robertson/Online Transport Archive*

1907: No. 16, Albert Drive, 11 August 1959. One of nine water tank/scrub cars built by the Corporation, most of which had 60hp motors fitted in the 1950s. It was sold in October 1962. *Hamish Stevenson/Online Transport Archive*

1937: No. 34, Langside depot, 1956. One of five Sett Wagons (33-37) built by the Corporation. It was scrapped in March 1958. *Frank Hunt/LRTA (London Area)/Online Transport Archive*

1939: No. 39, Admiral Street, 1951. Cars 38 and 39 were constructed at Coplawhill to deliver dry sand (hence the tarpaulin) to various depots. Special low-height cabs enabled them to access the interior of the sand drying plant on Admiral Street. Receiving equipment from scrapped cars in 1951, they were the only works cars to regularly appear in daylight. No. 38 was withdrawn in 1958 and No. 39 in 1959. *John Cadisch/Online Transport Archive*

GLASGOW CORPORATION TRAMWAYS
1 JANUARY 1948

Some peak hour services, shipyard specials and other extras not shown

Continued below

15·23 AIRDRIE

Coatbridge

C

Coatdyke

X

15·23 LANGLOAN

X'

same scale as main map

Depots	
C	Coatbridge
Dk	Dalmarnock
De	Dennistoun
E	Elderslie
G	Govan
L	Langside
M	Maryhill
N	Newlands
Ph	Parkhead
Pk	Partick
Pp	Possilpark

Other facilities	
CW	Coplawhill Works
AS	Admiral Street Sand Dryer

Glasgow City boundary

11 MILNGAVIE

20 DUNTOCHER

Hillfoot

Canniesburn

1·6·9·26 DALMUIR WEST

9·26 CLYDEBANK

20 CLYDEBANK

28 RENFREW FERRY

27 RENFREW CROSS

4 RENFREW SOUTH

River Clyde

1 SCOTSTOUN WEST

30 KNIGHTSWOOD

21·24 ANNIESLAND

6·9·16·26 SCOTSTOUN

17 WHITEINCH

13 MARYHILL

M

13·23·40 GAIRBRAID AVENUE

5·5A·10 KELVIN-SIDE

22 LAMBHILL

25 BISHOPBRIGGS

18 27 33

18·19·25·27 SPRINGBURN

Pp

4·16 KEPPOCHHILL ROAD

2·32 PROVANMILL

7·8 MILLERSTON

11·13·18 23·33·40

5A

1·10·30

Garngad

6·7·8 RIDDRIE

6·7 ALEXANDRA PARK

Pk

27 SHIELDHALL

12 LINTHOUSE

Ibrox

De

1 DENNISTOUN

1·7·23·30·34

Shettleston

15·23 BAILLIESTON

Bargeddie

X

Garrowhill

X'

21·32 ELDERSLIE

E

Paisley

7 BELLAHOUSTON

G

AS

22 CROOKSTON

3 MOSSPARK

40 DUMBRECK

CW

34 PARKHEAD CROSS

Dk

Ph

9 LONDON ROAD

Mount Vernon

Continued above

Broomhouse

9 CARMYLE

29 TOLLCROSS

9 AUCHENSHUGGLE

Glenfield

14·14A POLLOKSHAWS

24 LANGSIDE

2 POLMADIE

12·13 MOUNT FLORIDA

10·10A·18·26 RUTHERGLEN

17·30 CAMBUSLANG

Eastfield

⊖ = 5·5A•11·24

N

Newlands

L

11 SINCLAIR DRIVE

18·26 BURNSIDE

29 UDDINGSTON

Cross Stobs

25 CARNWADRIC

Thorniebank

19 NETHERLEE

Barrhead

14·14A·28 SPIERSBRIDGE

Eastward Toll

8·25 ROUKEN GLEN

8 GIFFNOCK

5·5A•13 CLARKSTON

0 ¼ ½ ¾ 1   2   3 miles
0   500   1000 yards
0   1   2   3   4   5 kilometres

Based on J C Gillham original, 1958
Drawn by R A Smith, 2021
Adapted for this volume by Charles Roberts

N
W E
S

1948

Unfortunately, 1948 did not start well.

11 April 1948: Parts of the largest depot, Newlands, were damaged by fire. Twenty-two passenger cars were destroyed or badly burnt, of which five were later repaired together with preserved horse car 543.

Above left: Several cars, including 1241 (second from right) suffered external scorching but were returned to service. *Michael H. Waller/Online Transport Archive*

Left: 1141, 1148, 1239 and 1272 were given new, less luxurious, replacement Coronation bodies, the last entering service in May 1951. Also destroyed at Newlands was the specially built-hex-dash *Kelvin Hall* decorated car No. 50 which is seen with slogans advertising a 'Safety Week'. *Bob Docherty collection/Online Transport Archive*

Above right: **Coronation Mark II**. 1948-52: **1293-1392**. Built at Coplawhill on inside frame Maley & Taunton bogies and fitted with four 36hp Metro-Vick motors, these proved more economical and easier to maintain than the Coronations. However, passengers disliked the narrow doors and the three steps up from the street. Furthermore, the lower saloons were cramped. Prone to pitch and roll until improvements were made, they were nicknamed 'Cunarders'. This view shows two under construction. Note the Standard displaying service number 35. *John A. Clarke/Online Transport Archive*

29 August 1948: Although the Corporation appeared committed to retaining the core system, concerns were mounting over lightly-trafficked sections also covered by faster competing bus routes. A case in point was the eastern limit of service 29 where few people used the trams on the two-mile section between Broomhouse (Calderpark Zoo) and Uddingston. Furthermore, the track was badly affected by subsidence. This, coupled with a dispute with Lanarkshire County Council, hastened the closure. **Track abandoned:** Broomhouse to Uddingston.

Left: 1209, Glasgow Road, 1948. The driver of this Coronation is obeying the 8mph speed restriction as the car picks its way cautiously along the sunken rails. *R.R. Clark/Scottish Tramway & Transport Society*

Below: 382, Uddingston Main Street, 1948. Although there was no physical connection, the town had been served by Lanarkshire Tramways until 1931. This Standard was withdrawn in early 1955. *F.N.T. Lloyd-Jones/Online Transport Archive*

3 October 1948: New track: To eliminate hold-ups on the main Paisley-Renfrew road, a long siding was opened on Porterfield Road. Known as Renfrew South, it became the terminus for service 4 and the starting point for 'specials' catering for the evening exodus from Babcock & Wilcox's Boiler Works.

7 November 1948: New track: 600 yard street track extension along Boydstone Road to Carnwadric which from 20 February 1950 became one of the southern termini of service 25.

Above: **129, Porterfield Road, 13 July 1956.** By now, most 4s terminated at Paisley North but at peak times, some still short-worked to Renfrew South. *C.C. Thornburn*

Left: **585, Boydstone Road, August 1950.** This former green car was purchased by a student from Leeds University in the Autumn of 1961 and now forms part of the Science Museum collection although it is not on public view. *R.W.A. Jones/Online Transport Archive*

Right: **741, Porterfield Road, 1949.** This former blue car was one of 40 Standards equipped with regenerative braking in 1935 and assigned to Govan and Possilpark depots. Although fitted with conventional controllers during 1949/50, these 'Regens' were among the first High-Speed Standards to be scrapped with 741 being withdrawn in June 1951. *F.N.T. Lloyd-Jones/Online Transport Archive*

1949

Although two extensions were opened, this year marked the beginning of the end for the tramway when services using the High Street, Saltmarket, Crown Street corridor were converted to trolleybus operation. The conversion of service 2 was said to be experimental but wiring was swiftly removed and junctions modified. Any prospect of a modern light rail network ended when the Transport Committee failed to approve General Manager E.R.L. Fitzpayne's recommendation that 10 Cunarders should be constructed as high-capacity, centre-entrance single-deckers so they could be evaluated on one route. At the beginning of June, peak demand was for 945 cars to operate the 297½ mile system.

23 January 1949: service 10 re-routed and service 10A discontinued. Some cars on service 26 diverted along Rutherglen Main Street to Oatlands as partial replacement for the 10. **Track abandoned**: Rutherglen Road (Crown Street to Shawfield).

19 February 1949: Former white services 2 (Provanmill to Polmadie – 4½ miles, 28 minutes) and 19 (Springburn to Netherlee – 6½ miles, 39 minutes) temporarily replaced by buses. **Track abandoned**: Royston Road, High Street, Saltmarket, Crown Street. **Last car**: 494 (Polmadie-Provanmill-Possilpark depot).

444, Rutherglen Main Street. A rare view of a 10 in Rutherglen. A former red car, it lasted until December 1956. *R.R. Clark/Scottish Tramway & Transport Society*

SERVICE PROFILE: 2, 19

As post-war scenes on these services are virtually non-existent, two pre-war views have been included to provide a flavour of the central area served.

Provanmill, 1948. Car nearest the camera is on the long cross-city service 32 to Elderslie which was diverted to terminate at Springburn or Bishopbriggs. *F.N.T. Lloyd Jones/ Online Transport Archive*

459, Provanmill, 19 February 1949. Passengers appear to be boarding away from the regular stop and the bow collector has not yet been flipped over. *R.R. Clark/Scottish Tramway & Transport Society*

Above: **51, Glasgow Cross, junction with Argyle Street.** *G.W. Price collection*

Left: **High Street** with Barony North United Reformed Church (left) and Royal Infirmary (right). *G.W. Price collection*

Below left: **1071, Aikenhead Road, 12 September 1947.** During 1949/50, these ex-Paisley cars migrated back to Elderslie depot. *John H. Meredith/Online Transport Archive*

Below right: **1070, Polmadie, 6 July 1946.** This car and 1071 (left) were both withdrawn from Elderslie in November 1951. *A.D. Packer*

Polmadie, 1948. Note the gated entrance into the North British Locomotive Co. Ltd., works. *F.N.T. Lloyd-Jones/Online Transport Archive*

Cathcart Road/Aikenhead Road junction, 8 June 1948. The car on service 2 is about to turn towards the city whilst the 19 is outbound for Mount Florida. *B.J. Cross collection/Online Transport Archive*

417, Cathcart Road/Allison Street junction, 19 February 1949. This former red car only survived until the summer of 1956. *R.R. Clark/Scottish Tramway & Transport Society*

Clarkston Road, near Netherlee, 1948. *F.N.T. Lloyd-Jones/Online Transport Archive*

2 April 1949: Concerted local opposition failed to stop closure of a mile-long stretch of the former Paisley District interurban to Spiersbridge where connection was made with the Glasgow system. This rural section had been under threat since 1947 when Renfrewshire Road Board condemned the track formation as dangerous, declaring that Caplethill Road had to be rebuilt with double track. Knowing the farebox could not recoup the estimated £20,000 outlay, Glasgow suggested continuing the service until the track was life-expired but Renfrew held firm so, much to the annoyance of Barrhead Town Council who resented the loss of a through service to Paisley, it was agreed to close the section. **Track abandoned:** Glenfield to Cross Stobs – single track with three loops.

SECTION PROFILE: GLENFIELD TO CROSS STOBS

Caplethill Road/Brownside loop, 1949. This was one of over 130 Semi-High Speed Standards. Powered by just two 45hp motors, they were restricted to about 23mph on level track, hardly ideal for a hilly route like the 28. It is hard to believe such low powered cars were assigned to Glasgow's longest route which from October 1934 to August 1943 linked Renfrew Ferry to Milngavie, a staggering 22¾ miles for just 2½d. Every effort was made to keep these under-powered cars away from the city to avoid delays but they were retained on the 28 as the power supply from the Barrhead sub-station was sometimes below par and struggled when coping with more powerful cars. *N.N. Forbes/ National Tramway Museum*

1063/965, Brownside loop, 1949. After Glasgow took over Paisley District in 1923, the road under the bridge in the background was lowered to accommodate totally-enclosed double-deckers and the associated loop quadrupled in length. The absence of street lights on this exposed section would have been hazardous at night especially during driving rain, winter blizzards and war-time blackout. 965, which had once been fitted with experimental Swiss motors, was withdrawn in the November and ex-Paisley District 1063 in June 1952. *Michael H. Waller/ Online Transport Archive*

909, Caplethill Road/Hilltop loop. Movements through the loops were controlled by signals, contactors in the overhead operating the signals and the points. To ensure accurate activation, drivers had to stop at studs positioned between the rails. *N.N. Forbes/National Tramway Museum*

921, Caplethill Road/Little loop. This short, aptly named loop, had very sharp turnouts. *F.N.T. Lloyd-Jones/Online Transport Archive*

1063, Caplethill Road South End, Cross Stobs, 24 March 1949. As Caplethill Road was already served by frequent competing buses, the rush hour replacement provided by the Corporation between Paisley Cross and Barrhead was short-lived. Although wires and track were swiftly removed, the road was not rebuilt for many years. From 3 April 1949, service 14 was extended to Cross Stobs from Spiersbridge. *Michael H. Waller/Online Transport Archive*

1063/648, Spiersbridge, 24 March 1949. This was the one-time limit of Paisley District operations and was, until 2 April 1949, the terminus of the 28 from Paisley and the 14 from Glasgow. 648 and 1063 were withdrawn in April 1957 and June 1952 respectively. *Michael H. Waller/Online Transport Archive*

31 July 1949: **New track:** Service 30 extended just under a mile from Knightswood Cross to Blairdardie.

SECTION PROFILE:
BLAIRDARDIE EXTENSION

Great Western Road/Knightswood Cross, 1949. Extension under construction.
F.N.T. Lloyd-Jones/Online Transport Archive

584, Knightswood Cross, 12 September 1947. This car, which lasted until September 1952, is going to Cambuslang which was served by the 30 from April 1945 to January 1949. *John H. Meredith/Online Transport Archive*

400, Blairdardie, May 1955. The extension was on central reservation in the middle of a steadily climbing dual carriageway with centre poles supporting the overhead. Originally intended to reach Duntocher, these plans were thwarted by the presence of the bridge over the Forth & Clyde Canal. *Ray DeGroote/Online Transport Archive*

2 September 1949: Airdrie terminus relocated to the western side of the busy A73 road junction on Clark Street.

1154, Forrest Street, Airdrie, 1948. Terminus prior to relocation. *F.N.T. Lloyd-Jones/Online Transport Archive*

4 December 1949: Replacement of service 20 Clydebank-Duntocher – 2¼ miles, 13 minutes. This double-track 'branch' off Dumbarton Road only opened in the mid-1920s. It featured a steep grade, open country, industrial premises, a canal swing bridge and a very low railway bridge dictating the use of single-deckers. **Track abandoned:** entire line. **Last car:** believed to be 1022.

SERVICE PROFILE: 20

Above left: **1037, Duntocher, 1939.** Note the Hosiery Mill destroyed in the Clydeside blitz. *R.T. Coxon/ Hamish Stevenson collection*

Above right: **821/1013, Duntocher, 1948.** At the height of the blitz on 13 March 1941, three trams were driven here for refuge. The cars and crew survived but the 20 was suspended from 14 March to 4 May 1941. The three stranded trams were later removed by road to Partick depot. On their descent, the 'wee caurs' picked up workers employed at the nearby Singer sewing-machine factory. An intense peak hour headway resulted in frequent bunching. *F.N.T. Lloyd-Jones/ Online Transport Archive*

Right: **1022, Parkhall, 1948.** At times of peak demand there were even some short working cars on the 2¼ mile service. *F.N.T. Lloyd-Jones/Online Transport Archive*

1024, Kilbowie Road, 23 August 1947. Residential properties flanked the steep grade.

J.L. Stevenson/Online Transport Archive

1024, Kilbowie Road, 1948. Note the 'Stop Clear of the Gates' sign, the section boxes and the iron work supporting the overhead when this swing bridge (1915) over the Forth & Clyde Canal was open. *F.N.T. Lloyd-Jones/Online Transport Archive*

Kilbowie Road, 1949. Catch points guarding the approach to the canal bridge (far distance) were activated from the bridge control cabin, which ensured a tram would derail if it overshot the 'All Cars Stop' sign. Once the bridge was repositioned, the points were reset. In the background is one of the two low railway bridges. *B.J. Cross collection/Online Transport Archive*

1011, Clydebank, 24 March 1949. Passengers can be seen filling the bench seat on the platform. *Michael H. Waller/Online Transport Archive*

Above: 1018, Kilbowie Road, Clydebank, 24 March 1949. A conductress uses a point iron to change the points ready for the car to head north again. Working such a well-used service with low capacity two-man single-deckers was hardly economical and at peak times people were often left waiting. *Michael H. Waller/Online Transport Archive*

Left: 923, Kilbowie Road, Clydebank. To avoid causing delays when working to and from Partick depot, the under-powered 'Tocher' single-deckers were sometimes towed in and out of service by Standards or Kilmarnock bogies. Note the side destination screen on these cars. Only 1017 survived this closure. *G.F. Ashwell/Online Transport Archive*

1950/51

In May 1951, total mileage stood at some 293 with a peak demand for 908 out of a fleet of 1164. In October 1951, the condition of 621 cars was said to be 'good' or 'very good', 56 'bad' and in need of urgent withdrawal and, perhaps most worryingly, 487, equal to just under a third of the fleet, as only 'fair'. Although some were being replaced by the new Cunarders, certain councillors challenged the ongoing commitment to tramway retention by advocating further expansion of the trolleybus network. Furthermore, the Inglis Report of 1951 on the future of transport in the Greater Glasgow area advocated electrification of much of the suburban rail network alongside replacement by various nationalised bus companies of many tram services extending beyond the city boundary.

1 July 1951: In readiness for the introduction of trolleybuses on the Glassford, Stockwell and Gorbals Streets corridor service 11 (Milngavie-Sinclair Drive – 10 miles, 56 minutes) was replaced by buses and services 5, 5A and 24 were re-routed via Glasgow Bridge. Service 13, which continued to use the corridor, was extended to Milngavie to replace the 11 whilst in the south some 24s were diverted to serve Sinclair Drive until new service 24A took over this southern prong as from 5 August. Service 11 was worked from Maryhill and Langside depots by Standards and Coronations. **Track abandoned:** Pollokshaws Road between Gorbals Street and Turriff Street.

PROFILE: SERVICE 11 AND POLLOKSHAWS ROAD

Right: **223, West Nile Street, May 1951.** Note the banner-carrying procession in the distance. *W.J. Wyse/LRTA (London Area)/Online Transport Archive*

Below left: **1211, Milngavie, 1948.** *F.N.T. Lloyd-Jones/Online Transport Archive*

Below right: **742, St Vincent Place, east end, 1949.** Eglinton Toll is wrongly spelt on the destination screen of 742 which is passing a British Road Services Fordson lorry. *C. Carter/Online Transport Archive*

Above left: 146, George Square approaching South Frederick Street, 21 June 1951. *C. Carter*

Above right: 1286, Stockwell Street, 1949. The Coronation is about to cross Victoria Bridge. During World War II, many of this type had longitudinal seating fitted in the lower saloon to create more space for standees. *C. Carter*

Left: 1222, Sinclair Drive, 1948. This third of a mile spur off Grange Road served an older residential part of Langside. *F.N.T. Lloyd-Jones/Online Transport Archive*

2 December 1951: Short-lived service 24A replaced by buses. **Track abandoned**: Sinclair Drive.

521, Sinclair Drive, 1951. This view shows the whole length of the short spur.

C.C. Thornburn collection

1952

Another relatively stable year. In May, 904 cars were required to operate the 282¾ mile network. Coronation Mark II No. 1392 entered service on 13 February and was the last new double-deck tram to be built by GCT.

4 May 1952: Service 34 (Anderston Cross-Auchenshuggle – 4½ miles) discontinued. One of several services introduced after the war to provide additional capacity on trunk corridors which by March 1951 basically duplicated the eastern section of service 9. **Track abandoned:** None.

15 June 1952: Service 9 cut back from Carmyle to relocated terminus at Auchenshuggle. The Auchenshuggle-Mount Vernon section built to relieve unemployment in the 1920s was little used until May 1944 when some journeys on service 9 were extended from Auchenshuggle to Carmyle, a distance of about two-thirds of a mile. **Track abandoned:** London Road between Causewayside Street and Tollcross Road at Mount Vernon.

SECTION PROFILE: LONDON ROAD

Right: **22, Auchenshuggle, 1951.** Seen on service 34, this car survives today at the National Tramway Museum. *C.C. Thornburn collection*

Below left: **363, Carmyle, 1951.** During term-time, a few schools 'specials' continued beyond here to terminate about a mile away on a short length of single track near Kenmuirhill Road. *C.C. Thornburn collection*

Below right: **466, London Road.** Crossing the railway bridge over the former Caledonian Railway line from Baillieston. Note Colville's steel works on the right. Some redundant wiring from this section was reused on the growing trolleybus system. *R.R. Clark/Scottish Tramway & Transport Society*

1953

Maximum turn-out in May required 899 cars to operate the 277¾ mile tramway. Concerns over the loss of short stage revenue led the Corporation to reject proposals to surrender operation of tram routes outside its boundaries to Scottish Omnibuses. Preparations well advanced for the Clarkston conversion to trolleybuses. Purchase of 24 cars from Liverpool agreed at a cost of £500 each including transportation. Last ex-Paisley District cars withdrawn with 1068 set aside for preservation.

11 January 1953: To enable tram and trolleybus overhead to exist side by side, the siding at the busy city centre terminus at St Vincent Place was removed and various short-workings relocated to nearby crossovers.

19 April 1953: Service 1 extended from Dennistoun to Dalmarnock. Owing to restricted curves at Parkhead Cross, bogie cars continued to appear occasionally on service 1 but only as far as Dennistoun.

Above left: **St Vincent Place, 1948.** *F.N.T. Lloyd-Jones/Online Transport Archive*

Above right: **1274, Great Western Road, 1952.** This car was despatched to the Seashore Trolley Museum in the USA on 11 September 1963. *G.W. Morant/ Online Transport Archive*

Right: **1189, George Square, 21 June 1951.** This was the first Coronation to have its upper deck drop-down windows at either end replaced by solid panes including a small aperture to access the bow rope. *C. Carter*

19 April 1953: Service 36 (Kelvinside and Parkhead Circle – 11½ mile round trip) withdrawn without replacement. Introduced in January 1949 and worked entirely by Standards from Partick and Dalmarnock depots, it ran from Kelvinside through the city from where it transcribed an anti-clockwise circle via Bridgeton Cross, Dalmarnock Road, Springfield Road, Parkhead Cross and Gallowgate. **Track abandoned:** None.

SERVICE PROFILE: 36

Above: **64, Charing Cross, 1951.** Negotiating the newly realigned track. *W.D. McMillan/ Travel Lens Photographic*

Above right: **333, Hope Street/Gordon Street, 1952.** *A.W.V. Mace/National Tramway Museum*

Right: **581, Kelvinside, 1952.** *TLRS Archive*

5 July 1953: Introduction of trolleybus service 105 led to creation of new service 13 (Milngavie or Maryhill to Glasgow Cross) plus curtailment of the 5/5A at Holmlea Road, Langside. Service 23 re-routed via Cambridge Street and New City Road. **Track abandoned:** Parts of Garscube Road and Cowcaddens as well as West Nile Street, George Square south; South Frederick, Glassford, Stockwell and Gorbals Streets, Cathcart Road (except between Allison Street and Mount Florida), Cathcart Road/Holmlea Road junction to Clarkston.

SECTION PROFILE: CITY CENTRE CLOSURES

1210, Garscube Road, junction with Possil Road/St George's Road, April 1953. Service 23 had used this routing since January 1947. This car was one of many destroyed in a depot fire at Dalmarnock in March 1961. *R.J.S. Wiseman/National Tramway Museum*

486, Cowcaddens Street, near Buchanan Street station, 21 June 1951. *C. Carter/Online Transport Archive*

31, George Square south, 1949. *C. Carter*

241, Stockwell Street, approaching Victoria Bridge, May 1951. This car has been recently out-shopped. *W.J. Wyse/LRTA (London Area)/Online Transport Archive*

Victoria Bridge, May 1951. Built on the site of an early crossing, this structure dates from 1854. Note the two mounted policemen on the right. *W.J. Wyse/LRTA (London Area)/Online Transport Archive*

Above: **463**, Cathcart Road/Holmlea Road, May 1951. Langside depot can be seen in the distance. *W.J. Wyse/LRTA (London Area)/Online Transport Archive*

Below: **650**, Clarkston Road railway bridge looking towards Holmlea Road, **July 1952.** Note the warning 10mph speed restriction plate attached to the wires. *R.W.A. Jones/Online Transport Archive*

991, Cathcart Road, July 1952. This car only survived two more years. *R.W.A. Jones/Online Transport Archive*

663, Clarkston Road/Couper Institute Hall (1924), July 1952. This former white car was in traffic until July 1954. *R.W.A. Jones/Online Transport Archive*

212, Clarkston Road/City Boundary, July 1952. Note the white band on the traction pole indicating a section point. Note trolleybus wiring incomplete. *R.W.A. Jones/Online Transport Archive*

850, Clarkston Road. Muirend, July 1952. *R.W.A. Jones/Online Transport Archive*

663, Netherlee, 10 August 1952. *R.B. Parr/Scottish Tramway & Transport Society*

447, Clarkston Road railway bridge, July 1952. Note the track spacing over the narrow bridge. *R.W.A. Jones/Online Transport Archive*

776, Clarkston Toll, c1950. Car withdrawn May 1953. *Geoff Smith collection*

881, Mearns Road, Clarkston, 1950. Withdrawn in May 1959, the car was mounted on this EMB truck from 1935 to 1956. *R.W.A. Jones/Online Transport Archive*

4/1160, Mearns Road/Clarkston. July 1952. Conveniently located off the main road, the terminal stub was used by services 5, 5A and 13. *R.W.A. Jones/Online Transport Archive*

4 October 1953: In order to accommodate the longer ex-Liverpool cars, service 29 was reorganised to become a 13¼ mile heavyweight linking Broomhouse to Milngavie in just under 70 minutes. Service 13 (Glasgow Cross to Maryhill or Milngavie) discontinued.

SERVICE PROFILE: 13

609/124, Milngavie Road, 30 May 1952. Note conductress changing the screen on 609 whilst 124 is only working as far south as Mount Florida. *John H. Meredith/Online Transport Archive*

1257, Maryhill Road/Forth & Clyde Canal aqueduct, July 1952. *R.W.A. Jones/Online Transport Archive*

766, West Nile Street, 4 April 1948. The legendary Glasgow Empire (1897, since demolished) was active until 1973. *Michael H. Waller/Online Transport Archive*

999/1203, Argyle Street, 1953. This view was taken shortly before service 13 disappeared and the 29 was extended to Milngavie. *A.D. Packer*

Ex-Liverpool 'Green Goddesses'. Delivered between October 1953 and April 1954, these 78-seat streamliners had Maley & Taunton swing-link bogies, air brakes and four 35hp motors. Bodies left Liverpool on a Saturday morning arriving at Coplawhill mid-day Monday where they were reunited with their newly re-gauged trucks which had come north a few days earlier. Whilst Liverpool was relieved to be rid of their 'troublesome Maleys', staff at Coplawhill were shocked by their poor condition. Built 1936: **1006-1016/1018-1030**.

Liverpool 927 (1024), Glasgow Cross, 5 September 1953. On arrival, the heavy bumpers were removed and trafficators, external mirrors, new lifeguards, Glasgow style couplings and bow collectors fitted. Power and lighting circuits were rewired and Coronation style lighting fitted inside.

City Centre, late 1953. In white undercoat, a Goddess undergoes night-time clearance tests which ultimately restricted them to seven possible services. Track layouts at some depots also presented problems.

1006, Milngavie, 16 October 1953. This view is believed to have been taken on the day the first Goddesses entered service.

1015, Barrhead, December 1953. This newly painted car is captured on a test run from Coplawhill to Cross Stobs. Later changes included an upper deck front window aperture to access the bow rope as well as seat and window replacements due to water ingress.

Ian Maclean (all)

1954

For the year ending 31 May 1954 there were officially 1067 trams in stock of which 852 were required to work the 267¾ mile network. Of the 57 cars scrapped during the financial year, some were replaced by the Liverpool cars of which a further 22 were delivered between May and November at a cost of £580 each including transportation. These had a mix of EMB lightweight and heavyweight trucks with the first two entering service towards the end of the year. The workload at Coplawhill meant the last did not enter service until May 1956 by which time it was claimed each was costing £1,200 to put into service.

6 February 1954: Unable to accommodate the longer Goddesses, the stub terminus at Maryhill, was used for the last time. **Track abandoned:** Caldercuilt Road.

7 February 1954: New crossover installed a quarter of a mile to the north-west on a wide part of Maryhill Road.

Above left: **28, Caldercuilt Road siding, May 1951.** *W.J. Wyse/LRTA (London Area)/Online Transport Archive*

Above right: **1037, Maryhill Road/new terminus, 21 May 1955.** Seen on its first day in service, this Goddess was active for under four years. *Ray DeGroote/Online Transport Archive*

Right: **886 (later 1042), Kilmarnock Road, 23 August 1954.** Towed from Coplawhill by 364, the car is about to be shunted into Newlands depot for storage. After finally entering service in June 1955, it was the first Goddess to be withdrawn in August 1957. *R.J.S. Wiseman/National Tramway Museum*

Replacement Mark I Coronations. Financed mostly by insurance money from the Newlands depot fire, this 'fiery' sextet was built to a less costly specification than the original Coronations. They also had trucks, motors and equipment salvaged following a depot fire in Liverpool. Then, in a quirk of fate, four would go up in smoke in yet another depot fire in March 1961. Similar replacement bodies were built for two Coronations – also fire victims! 1954: **1393-1398 and 1279**; 1955: **1255**.

Right: **1393, Mosspark Boulevard, July 1954.** Together with 1395-1397, this car was destroyed by fire at Dalmarnock depot. *Phil Tatt/Online Transport Archive*

Left: **1394, Newlands depot, 8 August 1954.** When this view was taken, 1394 had been service just four days. Together with 1393 and 1395 it later received trucks and motors from withdrawn Coronations. When those from 1395 were transferred to 1398 after the Dalmarnock fire, the Liverpool sound was finally silenced. The Goddess is on an enthusiasts' tour. *R.R. Clark/Scottish Tramway & Transport Society*

19 September 1954: A new coup (tip) opened by the Permanent Way department at Colston. Used at night to off-load redundant setts and rubble and by day to burn withdrawn Standards until stopped by the fire brigade.

9 October 1954: To improve reliability and timekeeping, service 21 (Anniesland-Elderslie) cut back to terminate at St Vincent Street; service 25 (Rouken Glen-Bishopbriggs) cut back to Colston (Hillcroft Terrace) and service 32 (Bishopbriggs to Elderslie) cut at Crookston. Service 17 reorganised to operate between Anniesland and Cambuslang.

Above left: **No. 33, Colston coup, 1954.** New in 1937, this sett wagon survived until 1959 when the coup was closed. *Barry Cross collection/Online Transport Archive*

Above right: **480, Anniesland, 18 June 1949.** This car was an early casualty being scrapped in June 1955. *Michael H. Waller/Online Transport Archive*

Right: **422, Paisley High Street, 9 October 1954.** The Western SMT Utility Guy Arab is on a local Paisley route. *Ian M. Coonie/Graham Ewing collection/Online Transport Archive*

1955

20 March 1955: Service 25 re-extended from Colston to Bishopbriggs.

April 1955: It was agreed that 300 life-expired Standards should be scrapped. To achieve this, services 4, 5, 5A, 21, 22, 24, 27, 28 and 32 were to be replaced by buses and services 7 and 12 by trolleybuses. As a result, trams would disappear from Govan, Paisley and Renfrew. The depots at Elderslie, Govan and Possilpark would also close. At the end of May, 843 cars were still needed to operate the 256 mile network.

Above left: **431, George Square, May 1955.** Withdrawn in the November, this was one of the 300 cars earmarked for scrap.

Above right: **503, Arden, May 1955.** This car would survive until November 1957.

Left: **624, Glasgow Bridge, May 1955.** This car lasted until July 1956. By now many Standards needed internal body bracing. *Ray DeGroote/Online Transport Archive (all)*

6 August 1955: Some changes to services 18/26 prior to introduction of trolleybuses into the Royal Burgh of Rutherglen. **Track abandoned**: Main Street, Rutherglen and part of Glasgow Road, Rutherglen.

SECTION PROFILE: PARTS OF RUTHERGLEN

1095, Main Street, Rutherglen, 14 April 1955. Dominating the scene is the Royal Burgh's impressive Town Hall. *R.J.S. Wiseman/National Tramway Museum*

117, Glasgow Road, 4 August 1955. Both sides dominated by the giant Shawfield Chemical Works, closed in 1967. The railway connecting the two sites is in front of the tram. *R.J.S. Wiseman/National Tramway Museum*

452, Glasgow Road/Rutherglen Road, Shawfield, 4 August 1955. *R.J.S. Wiseman/National Tramway Museum*

172/359, Oatlands/Rutherglen Road. The entrance to Shawfield greyhound stadium is on the left. *G.W. Price collection*

7 August 1955: Services 18 and 26 rerouted. Service numbers 18A and 26A introduced for cars terminating at Shawfield where a new crossover was installed. Returning from here cars showed 18 or 26.

1956

In May, the network stood at 256 miles with 813 cars needed to meet the peak demand on the 32 numbered services, as well as the scheduled journeys without service numbers ('specials') and the many extras, but the axe was poised over several sections beyond the city boundary. Coatbridge and Langside depots closed. Track and fleet maintenance declined although overhauls and repaints still took place. In response to the Suez fuel crisis, the Paisley closures were postponed and night tram services reintroduced. Appeals for reinstatement of service 15 to Airdrie proved unsuccessful.

2 February 1956: Approval given for abandonment of selected 'beyond-the-boundary' services at a saving of £80,000 per annum as well as conversion of services 7 and 12 to trolleybuses. Cost of track lifting and road reinstatement estimated at £425,000.

8 May 1956: 1056, the last Goddess entered service.

13 September 1956: Council opposed complete abandonment.

29 September 1956: Southern 3½ mile limit of former blue service 14 (Cross Stobs-University) withdrawn without replacement. Worked from Newlands depot, this part of the former Paisley District system was described latterly as a 'white knuckle ride'. It featured an undulating roadside reservation, steep grades with regulatory Board of Trade stops, a level crossing with a single-track mineral railway, a tram-only bridge, tight bends and double track in a narrow country road. **Track abandoned:** Arden to Cross Stobbs.

SECTION PROFILE: ARDEN TO CROSS STOBS

1302, Nitshill Road side reservation, May 1955. *Ray DeGroote/Online Transport Archive*

1330, Nitshill Road/Darnley Bridge, 1956. *R.R. Clark/Scottish Tramway & Transport Society*

256, Darnley, October 1956. Site of a tragic runaway when a car toppled over resulting in three deaths. *J.G. Todd/Online Transport Archive*

1328, Darnley, 9 September 1956. Another accident but not so serious. Crew and police help to manhandle a damaged Morris Oxford off the track. *J. Venn*

Above: **1312, Princes Square, Barrhead. 5 July 1956.** *John A. Clarke*

Left: **Darnley Road, Parkhouse, 8 August 1954.** A good view of the double track occupying the full width of this country road. *W.G.S. Hyde/Online Transport Archive*

1306, Cross Arthurlie Street, Barrhead, 5 July 1956. *John A. Clarke*

1348, Barrhead Station, 1950. To challenge the trams directly, BR offered a range of cheap fares to and from Glasgow. *R.W.A. Jones/Online Transport Archive*

1306, Bellfield Street, Barrhead, 5 July 1956. The Leyland PD1 bus is from locally-based independent McGill's. *John A. Clarke*

311, Cross Stobs, May 1955. The abandoned line to Glenfield can be seen stretching off into the countryside. *Ray DeGroote/Online Transport Archive*

29 September 1956: Langside depot (capacity 130) closed to trams, its remaining allocation being transferred to Govan and Newlands, the former now covering all duties on service 12. Grange Road and Prospecthill Road no longer used by cars taking up service on the 12; however, the latter, accessed from Cathcart Road, remained available for football cars and it is possible it may have been used for driver training purposes.

Left: **Langside depot, 6 July 1956.** Note the spacious interior with its many wooden cleaning gantries. *John A. Clarke*

Below left: **888, Grange Road, 28 September 1956.** *W.A.C. Smith/Transport Library*

Below right: **693, Prospecthill Road, 19 April 1952.** The car at the rear of this football line-up survived just two more months. *Nigel McMillan*

3 November 1956: A black day in the annals of Glasgow trams with several long sections abandoned without direct replacement. The major loss involved the eastern limit of the 12¼ mile former green service 15 between Baillieston and Airdrie which was worked from Coatbridge and Parkhead depots. The abandoned 5½ mile section included all the former isolated Airdrie & Coatbridge system acquired by Glasgow in 1921 as well as the 2¼ mile roadside reservation built to link the two systems. Despite the introduction of through Airdrie-Glasgow trams, a local service continued to run between Airdrie and either Coatbridge or Langloan. These cars displayed either a split 15/23 or a blank screen. **Track abandoned**: Baillieston to Airdrie. **Last car:** 1251 (Airdrie-Baillieston-Coatbridge depot)

Right: **1251, last journey.** The car was watched by significant crowds as it made its final run during the early hours on the Sunday crewed by William Murdoch and Peggy Kearney. *G.W. Price collection*

SECTION PROFILE: AIRDRIE-BAILLIESTON

499, Airdrie, 1950. Glasgow contributed to the cost of track lifting and associated road works. *R.W.A. Jones/Online Transport Archive*

1147, Clark Street, Airdrie, 4 July 1956. By this time, Coronations were the mainstay on the interurban *John A. Clarke*

Above left: **20, Clark Street, east of Queen Victoria Street, Airdrie, 4 July 1956.** Since March, the Airdrie local had become part-day only. No. 20 was a long-time resident of Coatbridge depot. *John A. Clarke*

Above right: **1153, Alexander Street, Airdrie, 4 July 1956.** Note the old cottages. *John A. Clarke*

Below: **Deedes Street, Coatdyke.** Six Coronations held up following a collision in which a lorry shed coal over this busy intersection. *G.W. Price collection*

1186, Main Street, Coatbridge, 4 July 1956. Note the 'Wee Rovers' football ground. *John A. Clarke*

660, Main Street, Coatbridge. This car is close to the depot on service 23. *A.D. Packer*

673, Jackson Street, Coatbridge, August 1955. When the six-track depot closed, its five Standards and 16 Coronations were relocated. *E.C. Bennett & Martin Jenkins/Online Transport Archive*

1247, Main Street, Coatbridge, 4 July 1956. Note the chimneys of the Phoenix & Clifton iron works closed in 1967. Nearby was Connells of Coatbridge, the firm which scrapped Edinburgh and Glasgow trams. *John A. Clarke*

1229, Main Street, Coatbridge, October 1956. Both the Theatre Royal and Odeon cinemas have been demolished. *Ray Bicknese/courtesy Martin Jenkins/Online Transport Archive*

1186, Main Street, Coatbridge, east of Canal Street bridge, 4 July 1956. *John A. Clarke*

1162, Fountain, Coatbridge Central station, 7 July 1956. The road under the bridges was lowered in the 1920s but owing to the steep dip, a 5mph speed restriction applied to the trams. *A.D. Packer*

1184, West End Park, Coatbridge, 4 July 1956. *John A. Clarke*

1185, Drumpellier Terrace, Langloan, 4 July 1956. Much of the track on this key service had been put into good order in the late 1940s. This is one of a number of long-serving Coatbridge depot cars. *John A. Clarke*

1182, Langloan, July 1956. Note the loading island at the start of the reserved track section. Note also the 'no road' warning sign. *John A. Clarke*

1164, just east of Langloan, October 1956. Latterly, riding the reservation was quite 'rough'. *J.G. Todd/Online Transport Archive*

1162, approaching Bargeddie, May 1955. Based at Coatbridge, this Coronation is in almost original condition. *Ray DeGroote/Online Transport Archive*

166, Coatbridge Road, Bargeddie, 12 March 1945. Having toppled on its side, the car was righted and towed to Coatbridge depot by 1144. It survived in traffic until December 1958. *G.W. Price collection*

1163, Coatbridge Road/junction with the B757, 4 July 1956. This area changed considerably when the M8/M73 intersection was built. *R.R. Clark/Scottish Tramway & Transport Society*

1157, Coatbridge Road, Bargeddie. The crossover was used by cars short-working from the city. This car was one of those destroyed in the Dalmarnock depot fire of March 1961. *John A. Clarke*

1182, approaching Baillieston, 4 July 1956. Note the start of new housing development. Today there is virtually no trace of this roadside reservation with its centre poles and super-elevated curves. *John A. Clarke*

3 November 1956: Withdrawn without replacement was the 2¼ mile outer limit of former red service 17 (Anniesland-Cambuslang – 9 miles, 54 minutes). As the terminal stub in Cambuslang ('the largest village in Scotland') was unable to accommodate two trams if one was a bogie car, the all-street track 17 was worked by Standards from Dalmarnock and Partick depots. **Track abandoned:** Cambuslang to Farme Cross where a new crossover was installed close to the Clyde Paper Mill. **Last car:** 255

SECTION PROFILE: CAMBUSLANG-FARME CROSS

Above left: **684, Cambuslang Main Street, August 1955.** *Frank Hunt/LRTA (London Area)/Online Transport Archive*

Above right: **168, Cambuslang Main Street, 7 July 1956.** Crowds are observing a religious procession from the windows of the tall buildings flanking this narrow canyon of which little survives today. *John A. Clarke*

Left: **72/168, Main Street/Miller Street, 7 July 1956.** *John A. Clarke*

171, Ardoch Grove, 4 July 1956. This crossover was used by some peak hour cars from the city. *A.D. Packer*

72, Cambuslang Road, 7 July 1956. *John A. Clarke*

506, Cambuslang Road/Whinfield Avenue, 7 July 1956. Note the poor state of the setts surrounding the rails. *John A. Clarke*

394/677, Cambuslang Road, east of Rutherglen railway bridge, July 1956. The entrance to Rutherglen Goods Station is on the right. *John A. Clarke*

The same night also led to loss, without replacement, of the 3½ miles of street track at the northern end of the 29 (Broomhouse-Milngavie – 13¼ miles, 69 minutes). Running through prosperous residential areas, the last part of this hilly, undulating line had opened in 1934. By November 1956, the 29 was worked from Maryhill, Dalmarnock and Parkhead depots, mostly by Standards, Coronations and ex-Liverpool cars. Coincidentally, the later type were also involved in a closure in their home city on the same day – a unique occurrence? **Track abandoned**: Maryhill to Milngavie. **Last car**: believed to be 517 from Milngavie

SECTION PROFILE: MARYHILL-MILNGAVIE

Above left: **495, Canniesburn, Bearsden, 1956.** The Rio Cinema (1934-86) has since been demolished. *W.D. McMillan/Travel Lens Photographic*

Above right: **1015, Maryhill Road/ Kessington, May 1955.** Note the ornate Bearsden sub-station, now a public hall. *Ray DeGroote/Online Transport Archive*

Left: **1049, Milngavie Road/Hillfoot Station, 13 July 1956.** *John A. Clarke*

163, North Hillfoot, 13 July 1956. *John A. Clarke*

1034, Milngavie Road/Burnbrae, 13 July 1956. *John A. Clarke*

1036, Milngavie Road, May 1955. The rusting experimental Bennie Railplane structure can be seen on the right. When withdrawn in June 1960, this was the last Goddess to survive. *Ray DeGroote/Online Transport Archive*

389, Milngavie, 1953. This car was an early casualty being withdrawn in December 1954. *Frank Hunt/LRTA (London Area)/Online Transport Archive*

To complete the closures of 3 November 1956, service 40 (Maryhill to either Ibrox (6¾ miles, 39 minutes) or Dumbreck (8½ miles, 49 minutes)) was discontinued on economic grounds. Introduced in 1943 and operated from Maryhill and Govan depots, it ran Mondays to Saturdays only. **Track abandoned**: none.

SERVICE PROFILE: 40

355, Maryhill, May 1955. *Ray DeGroote/Online Transport Archive*

725, Maryhill Road, 16 August 1954. *R.J.S. Wiseman/National Tramway Museum*

697, Oswald Street. This 1899 Standard had clocked up 58 years of service when withdrawn in June 1957. *Hamish Stevenson collection*

522, Paisley Road West, 3 November 1956. This last day scene shows the car turning into Broomloan Road. *G.W. Price collection*

549, Broomloan Road, Ibrox, 13 April 1952. This lengthy spur with two crossovers was also used by football cars. Although it remained available until November 1958, it is not known when it was last used. *A.D. Packer*

1000, Mosspark Boulevard, 8 June 1953. This car was scrapped a few months later. *G.W. Price collection*

207, Mosspark Boulevard. With driver Robert Starrett at the controls, this hex-dash Standard had managed to jump the track. *G.W. Price collection*

409/604, Dumbreck, 4 May 1956. 409, which survived until February 1959, was given this new flush-sided body in 1946. *W.A.C. Smith/Transport Library*

6 November 1956: A request from Airdrie Council to restore the trams was rejected.

1957

When the Suez crisis eased and fuel rationing ended, permission was given to abandon the trams in Paisley and Renfrew and to make further inroads into the routes serving Langside. By May 31, the network had shrunk to 215 miles with a peak hour demand for 704 trams.

10 February 1957: To avoid trams crossing the busy Edinburgh Road, Baillieston terminus was relocated to a new crossover on Main Street.

30 March 1957: Temporary night tram services to Baillieston, Burnside, Maryhill, Tollcross and Yoker discontinued following the end of fuel rationing.

Right: **10, Baillieston, September 1958.** Cars going for scrap at Connells of Coatbridge continued using the unwired south track to access the start of the reservation where they could be uplifted onto a lorry. Relying on the handbrake, drivers freewheeled their doomed vehicles across Edinburgh Road. *A.D. Packer*

Below: **419/1170, Baillieston old terminus, 1950.** Since October 1954, this had been terminus for the 23. Seen on a short-working 15 to Bargeddie, 419 was scrapped in 1956. *R.W.A. Jones/Online Transport Archive*

GLASGOW
CORPORATION
TRAMWAYS
1 JANUARY 1957

Some peak hour services, shipyard specials and other extras not shown

Depots	
Dk	Dalmarnock
De	Dennistoun
E	Elderslie
G	Govan
M	Maryhill
N	Newlands
Ph	Parkhead
Pk	Partick
Pp	Possilpark

Other facilities	
CW	Coplawhill Works
AS	Admiral Street Sand Dryer

Glasgow City boundary

1·6·9·26 DALMUIR WEST
9·26 CLYDEBANK
30 BLAIRDARDIE
29 MARYHILL
25·32 BISHOPBRIGGS
22·31 LAMBHILL
7·8 MILLERSTON
1 SCOTSTOUN WEST
17·24 ANNIESLAND
23 GAIRBRAID AVENUE
5·5A·10 KELVINSIDE
4·16·18·18A·25·27·33 SPRINGBURN
28 RENFREW FERRY
27 RENFREW CROSS
6·16·26·26A SCOTSTOUN
28 RENFREW SOUTH
6·7·8 RIDDRIE
River Clyde
4 PAISLEY NORTH
12·27 SHIELDHALL
12 LINTHOUSE
Ibrox
6·7 ALEXANDRA PARK
1 DENNISTOUN
1·7·23·30
15·23 BAILLIESTON
21 ELDERSLIE
Paisley
22·32 CROOKSTON
3 MOSSPARK
7 BELLAHOUSTON
Shettleston
Garrowhill
9·10 LONDON ROAD
Mount Vernon
29 BROOMHOUSE
28 GLENFIELD
14 CROSS STOBS
24 LANGSIDE
18A·26A SHAWFIELD
29 TOLLCROSS
9 AUCHENSHUGGLE
12 MOUNT FLORIDA
1·30 DALMARNOCK
17 FARME CROSS
25 CARNWADRIC
31 MERRYLEE
5·5A HOLMLEA ROAD
18·26 BURNSIDE
Thornliebank
Barrhead
14 ARDEN
8·25 ROUKEN GLEN
8 GIFFNOCK

Based on J C Gillham original, 1958
Drawn by R A Smith, 2021
Adapted for this volume by Charles Roberts

0 ¼ ½ ¾ 1   2   3 miles
0   500 1000 yards
0   1   2   3   4   5 kilometres

11 May 1957: Hundreds of local people signed petitions to prevent closure of the Paisley and Renfrew services but to no avail. Withdrawn without replacement were former green interurban service 21 (Elderslie-St Vincent Street – 8 miles, 44 minutes) and Paisley local service 28 (Glenfield-Renfrew Ferry – 5¼ miles, 27 minutes). Also lost were many specials, short-workings and extras. Elderslie depot also closed. **Track abandoned:** All of line 28; Paisley Cross to Elderslie; everything west of Crookston and Hillington Road.

Last cars: 1267 (21, City-Elderslie),1283 (28, Renfrew Ferry-Glenfield-Elderslie depot), 1277 (28, Glenfield-Renfrew Ferry-Elderslie depot)

Above left: **1277, 12 May 1957.** Driver Jim McColl left the Ferry at 12.20am on the Sunday morning. Battling through boisterous crowds, it took him 55 minutes to reach the depot. 1277 was among some 20 trams to leave Elderslie a few hours later, Coronations going to Dalmarnock, Standards to Govan, Maryhill and Possilpark and Lightweights to Govan, although No. 6 was initially sent to Possilpark by mistake. *Charles Dick*

Above right: **847/1275, Elderslie paint shop, April 1957.** This Standard was the last car to be broken up here on 8 May 1957. Rebodied after the blitz of 1941, 1275 suffered fire damage in 1957 but survived until June 1962. *E.C. Bennett & Martin Jenkins/Online Transport Archive*

Left: **167/281, Elderslie depot, June 1956.** With six tracks to accommodate some 50 cars together with its own workshops, upgraded in the late 1940s, it was almost self-sufficient. A siding on the right led to the workshops and an open area where car bodies were burnt. Depot staff were friendly and often showed visitors round. *George Fairley/Online Transport Archive*

SECTION PROFILE: ELDERSLIE-CROOKSTON

409, Elderslie Road, 6 July 1956. Cars entering and leaving the depot on services 21 and 28 reversed outside where a driver is seen changing the points. *John A. Clarke*

160, Elderslie East, August 1951. The lowered roadway under the bridge was liable to flooding. *R.W.A. Jones/Online Transport Archive*

679, Elderslie terminus, October 1955. This was the terminus for service 21. 679 was the first of a small group of Standards given new post-war flush-sided bodies. It was withdrawn in April 1958. *Martin Jenkins/Online Transport Archive*

1283, Station Road, 6 July 1956. *John A. Clarke*

143, Ferguslie Walk, 6 July 1956. *John A. Clarke*

225, Carbrook Street, 6 July 1956. Note the '28' card in the upper deck window. *John A. Clarke*

430, Paisley West, April 1957. *John Cadisch/Online Transport Archive*

1321, Wellmeadow Street/High Street, April 1957. *John Cadisch/Online Transport Archive*

1001, High Street, 6 July 1956. Unpopular with crews, the five Lightweights were unreliable, slow and noisy and were usually restricted to peak hour duties on the variations of the 28. 1001 ended its operational days at Govan in early 1958. *John A. Clarke*

1342, High Street, April 1957. *John Cadisch/Online Transport Archive*

77, High Street/Gilmour Street, April 1957. To regulate the intense service, an inspector and a pointsman were often stationed at this major intersection. *John Cadisch/Online Transport Archive*

Paisley Cross, 3 June 1940. Note the loading island on St James Bridge (widened in 1929) and also the impressive Town Hall. The car is on the long 15 cross-Glasgow service to Airdrie, which was later cut back to Anderston Cross. *Martin Jenkins collection/Online Transport Archive*

1003, Gauze Street, 6 July 1956. This Lightweight had similar equipment to a Standard and retained the drop down front upper deck windows to the end. It last ran in service in early 1958. *John A. Clarke*

70, Williamsburgh, April 1957. *John Cadisch/Online Transport Archive*

929, Hawkhead Road, April 1957. This former High-Speed car is on a Sunday only 'special' catering for local church-goers. Cars working to and from this point often showed 28. *John Cadisch/Online Transport Archive*

1355, Glasgow Road, April 1957. The tracks here were off-set due to road widening. *John Cadisch/Online Transport Archive*

Known as 'The Goldmine', service 28 benefited from heavy traffic in both directions carrying office, shipyard, engineering and mill workers, businessmen, school children, churchgoers and shoppers. In its heyday, it ran every two to three minutes in peak hours requiring some 50 cars plus specials. Tramscapes included open country, steep grades, narrow streets, right angle bends, single track, signals and sidings.

SERVICE PROFILE: 28

891, Glenfield, 1953. The former line to Cross Stobs is visible in the background. *Frank Hunt/LRTA (London Area)/Online Transport Archive*

1275, Neilston Road, May 1955. This car had been rebodied following the 1941 Blitz. *Ray DeGroote/Online Transport Archive*

Neilston Road, near Glenfield, 6 July 1956. The single track sections on this southern prong from Paisley Cross were doubled between 1924 and 1931. *John A. Clarke*

146, Potterhill Station, 6 July 1956. *John A. Clarke*

73, Lochfield Road, May 1957. This part-way crossover was installed in 1950.
E.C. Bennett & Martin Jenkins/Online Transport Archive

1282, Neilston Road/Braids Road, 6 July 1956. Nearer to the centre of Paisley, the road narrowed. Note the older properties and rich variety of chimney pots. This car is now preserved at the National Tramway Museum. *John A. Clarke*

891, Neilston Road, May 1957. This car had only a few months left in service.
E.C. Bennett & Martin Jenkins/Online Transport Archive

1291, Neilston Road/Stock Street, 6 July 1956. *John A. Clarke*

182, Canal Street, 6 July 1956. *John A. Clarke*

260, St Mirren Street, April 1957. Elderslie depot clerk Jim Caldwell oversees the transfer of takings into the Bank of Scotland. This 'Bullion car' ran from the depot to County Square where it reversed. It then proceeded to St Mirren Street where it stopped on the grade to allow the money to be off-loaded. It continued to Orchard Street crossover where it again reversed in order to pick up the Elderslie staff, after which it ran to County Square where it reversed in order to head back to the depot. *John Cadisch/Online Transport Archive*

1264, St Mirren Street, April 1957. This view highlights the steep 1-in-12 gradient. *John Cadisch/Online Transport Archive*

206, Paisley Cross, 11 May 1957. On the last day a laden 21 crosses the 28 tracks. *George Fairley/Online Transport Archive*

1268, County Square, August 1951. This three-track layout with crossover dated from 1926. Note the RAF recruiting van and the bridge carrying the railway into Gilmour Street station. *R.W.A. Jones/Online Transport Archive*

1272, Old Sneddon Street, 6 July 1956. The former line to Abbotsinch turned to the left. Coronations 1266-1283 enjoyed a long association with Elderslie depot. Although badly damaged in the 1948 Newlands depot fire, 1272 was active until June 1962. *John A. Clarke*

1068, Abercorn Street. This preserved car visited the siding serving Paisley sub-station on an enthusiasts' tour. *R.R. Clark/Scottish Tramway & Transport Society*

1054, Weir Street, August 1951. This 20ft length of single track was the last example in all-day use on the Glasgow system. This car was withdrawn the following month. *R.W.A. Jones/Online Transport Archive*

182, Weir Street/Renfrew Road, 6 July 1956. Note the tight, restricted curve and array of railway signals. *John A. Clarke*

1277, Abercorn Station, 6 July 1956. School specials served this location until 1953. *John A. Clarke*

206, Paisley North, 1957. To cater for new housing, service 4 was extended here in 1950. *W.D. McMillan/Travel Lens Photographic*

182, Renfrew Road, 6 July 1956. This stretch near Renfrew Airport had been a narrow country lane until widened in 1949 after which it became a proper 'speed track' with trams easily outpacing competing buses on this busy corridor. *John A. Clarke*

1003, Porterfield Road, May 1956. Shortly after 5.30pm on weekday evenings a procession of cars packed with employees from Babcock & Wilcox boiler works left this siding. Most went towards Paisley, but a few made for Govan and beyond. *Frank Hunt/ LRTA (London Area)/Online Transport Archive*

1360, Renfrew Road/Porterfield Road, May 1956. *Frank Hunt/LRTA (London Area)/ Online Transport Archive*

1266, Canal Street/Renfield Street, Renfrew, 6 July 1956. Note the splendid Gothic style town hall. *John A. Clarke*

1277, Ferry Road, Renfrew, 6 July 1956. Note the Regal cinema and the goods branch down to the river. *John A. Clarke*

945, Renfrew Ferry, April 1949. To ease movements on and off the chain ferry, the track layout here was altered several times. *F.N.T. Lloyd-Jones/Online Transport Archive*

11 May 1957: Despite opposition from Renfrew Council, two further losses, without replacement, occurred when services 4 (Paisley North-Springburn – 11 miles, 62 minutes) and 27 (Renfrew Cross-Springburn – 8¾ miles, 53 minutes) were cut back to the city boundary at Hillington Road. **Last car:** 1365 (4 from Paisley North to Govan depot).

SECTION PROFILE: RENFREW CROSS-HILLINGTON ROAD

Above left: **190, Hairst Street, April 1957.** With Renfrew Town Hall as the backdrop, the car is bound for Paisley North. *W.D. McMillan/Travel Lens Photographic*

Above right: **672, Renfrew Cross, April 1957.** Service 27 terminated here whilst 4s turned south to Paisley North. *John Cadisch/Online Transport Archive*

Left: **553, Renfrew Road, 6 July 1956.** Note the former track on Old Renfrew Road last used in 1926 when this new alignment skirting King George V dock was opened. *John A. Clarke*

24 June 1957: City Council approve complete tram scrapping programme which General Manager Fitzpayne recommends should take place over 15 to 20 years.

2 August 1957: Dalhousie Street substation and connecting track closed.

16 November 1957: Worked latterly from Partick and Newlands depots, former yellow services 5 (Holmlea Road-Kelvinside via Hyndland Road – 6½ miles, 40 minutes) and 5A (Holmlea Road-Kelvinside via Botanic Gardens – 6½ miles, 44 minutes) connected middle class suburbs north and south of the river each with their own local shopping districts and parades of handsome tenements. **Track abandoned:** Holmlea Road, Battlefield Road and Grange Road. Byres Road retained for depot workings on services 1,10 and 30 and parts of Hyndland Road for specials on service 24. **Last cars:** 1189 (5, Holmlea Road-Kelvinside via Great Western Road-Hyndland Road-Partick depot); 658 (5A, Holmlea Road-Hyndland Road-Kelvinside-Great Western Road-Partick depot).

17 November 1957: A mistake! Although the 5/5A closed the previous night, 1324, assigned to a regular convoluted early Sunday morning special strayed onto Battlefield Road.

20, Dalhousie Street. These two unvestibuled works cars are seen looking towards New City Road. *G.W. Price collection*

■ SERVICE PROFILE: 5/5A

138, Battlefield Road, April 1957. Note the paved reserved track and the only scissors crossover on the system. *E.C. Bennett & Martin Jenkins/Online Transport Archive*

Above left: **1258, Grange Road, 7 July 1956.**
The severed track led onto Annan Street
and was formerly used by football cars.
John A. Clarke

Above right: **1215, Langside Road/Queens
Drive, 7 July 1956.** Note the elegant
apartment buildings. *John A. Clarke*

Left: **1239, Victoria Road/Coplaw Street,
7 July 1956.** This car, a Newlands fire victim,
survived until June 1962. *John A. Clarke*

Eglinton Toll, 1956. The barrier erected here in 1946 segregated traffic flows at this major junction. *Doug Fallwell*

889, Pollokshaws Road/Turriff Street, 7 July 1956. *John A. Clarke*

1241, Glasgow Bridge, May 1955. Severely damaged in the 1948 Newlands depot fire, 1241 lasted until June 1962. *Ray DeGroote/Online Transport Archive*

422, Renfield Street, May 1951. Seen displaying a yellow route band, this car survived until August 1958. *W.J. Wyse/LRTA (London Area)/Online Transport Archive*

1242, Dumbarton Road/Church Street, 13 July 1956. *John A. Clarke*

40, Hyndland Road, April 1957. *John Cadisch/Online Transport Archive*

130, Byres Road, May 1957. *E.C. Bennett & Martin Jenkins/Online Transport Archive*

235, Hyndland Road, 7 July 1956. 5s worked anti-clockwise to Hyndland Station whilst the 5As went clockwise via Hyndland Road. *John A. Clarke*

Above left: 341/72/1168, Hyndland Station/Kelvinside, 4 July 1956. On arrival 5As worked back to Holmlea Road as 5s via Great Western Road. *John A. Clarke*

Above right: 1211, **Great Western Road/Byres Road**. Note the AEC Regent V demonstrator bus on service 11, on hire to GCT. *Hamish Stevenson collection*

Right: 227, **Hillhead, 13 July 1956.** *John A. Clarke*

1958

In April, it was agreed the whole system was to be scrapped over a 12-15 year period. Some 650 trams and 12 services were to be replaced during the next three years whilst the remaining routes 3, 9, 15, 17, 18/18A, 26/26A, 29 and 31 would be worked by modern cars until the early 1970s. By 31 May, a daily turn-out of some 640 cars operated the remaining 87 route miles which by December had been reduced to 75, with 12 being outside the city boundary. The Phase 1 replacement of 450 Standards reached its conclusion when trams were removed from Langside and the densely-populated areas fringing the south side docks. Also closed to trams was George V Bridge (1928) and the Admiral Street sand dryer plant, although Govan depot continued to house cars awaiting scrap. Among other cars withdrawn were the five Lightweights and the first 'Goddesses'. Following the sale of Pinkston Power Station, the Corporation now paid more for electricity. The year ended with a revised scrapping programme to be completed within five years after statistics showed the trams had lost £577,000 during the financial year 1957/58. The final services were now to be the 9 and 26, and 3 and 31.

15 March 1958: Service 24 (Langside to Anniesland – 7¼ miles, 46 minutes) replaced. Worked latterly from Newlands and Partick by a mix of Standards, Coronations and Cunarders, it was the last service using Victoria Road on the south side and Byres Road/Clarence Drive on the north side. Partick depot workings on 1,10 and 30 re-routed. **Track abandoned:** Langside to Eglinton Street; Church Street, Byres Road, Highburgh Road, Clarence Drive. **Last car:** 420 (Langside-Anniesland-Partick depot).

■ SERVICE PROFILE: 24

Above: **220, Langside Road/Grange Road, 8 March 1958.** *Hamish Stevenson/Online Transport Archive*

Below left: **1277, Langside, April 1957.** Note Langside Battlefield Monument and the neo-classical frontage to Langside Hill Free Church. *John Cadisch/Online Transport Archive*

Below right: **296, Langside Road/Queens Drive, 6 July 1956.** This is an area rich in imposing architecture. *John A. Clarke*

85, Victoria Road/Eglinton Toll, 6 July 1956. Note the Plaza cinema and the car emerging from Turriff Street in the distance. *John A. Clarke*

298, Eglinton Street/Turriff Street, 6 July 1956. *John A. Clarke*

1242, Jamaica Street/Broomielaw, 1956. *Frank Hunt/LRTA (London Area)/Online Transport Archive*

1393, Sauchiehall Street, 1956. This car was lost in the Dalmarnock depot fire of March 1961. *M.J. Lea/LRTA (London Area)/Online Transport Archive*

1324, Hyndland Road/Clarence Drive, April 1957. *John Cadisch/Online Transport Archive*

349, Clarence Drive railway bridge, 13 July 1956. *John A. Clarke*

1219/1223, Clarence Drive/Churchill Drive, 13 July 1956. 1219 was the last to have half-drop cab windows whilst 1223 was rebuilt after being badly damaged by enemy action in March 1941. *John A. Clarke*

1148, Broomhill Cross, 13 September 1954. *R.J.S. Wiseman/National Tramway Museum*

Cross-city service 27 (Hillington Road-Springburn – 7¾ miles, 47 minutes) replaced. Worked from Govan and Possilpark by a mix of Standards and Cunarders, it carried heavy peak hour traffic to and from the south side docks and the many industrial premises in the Springburn area. **Track abandoned:** none.

■ SERVICE PROFILE: 27

Above: **161, Govan Road, 1957.** The car is running alongside Princes Dock.
W.D. McMillan/Travel Lens Photographic

Left: **549, Renfrew Road/Bogmoor Road, 22 February 1958.** The Bogmoor stub was a major departure point for eastbound shipyard specials. *Hamish Stevenson/ Online Transport Archive*

Below left: **265/672, Commerce Street, 28 July 1955.** *R.J.S. Wiseman/National Tramway Museum*

Below right: **643, George V Bridge, 1957.** This Rebuilt Standard was in traffic from November 1947 until June 1959. *Marcus Eavis/Online Transport Archive*

407/347, Hope Street, 1951. Both cars withdrawn during the summer of 1956.
R.W.A. Jones/Online Transport Archive

423/303, Mosshouse, 15 March 1958. *J.L. Stevenson*

1039, Saracen Cross, junction of Saracen Street/Balmore Road, 15 March 1958.
The conductress looks suitably startled by having her photo taken as the car enters the short section of Saracen Street only used by the 27 and cars working to and from Possilpark depot. *J.L. Stevenson*

538, Hawthorn Street. Note the former Eastfield loco shed roundhouse (now demolished). *Hamish Stevenson collection*

Grange Road and Prospecthill Road officially closed. This single track section had been used by cars taking up service from Langside depot on service 12 as well as by football cars serving nearby Hampden Park. On match days, cars lined up awaiting the final whistle. Latterly, convoys of cars from Newlands carried supporters until sometime in 1958.

Right: **393, Grange Road, Annan Street, Prospecthill Road junction, 11 August 1953. This car survived until October 1957.** *R.J.S. Wiseman/National Tramway Museum*

Below left: **235, Prospecthill Road. This car is at the rear of a football line-up.** *B.J. Cross collection/ Online Transport Archive*

Below right: **697, Prospecthill Road approaching junction with Cathcart Road, 11 July 1953. When withdrawn in June 1957, this car had clocked up 58 years of service.** *R.J.S. Wiseman/National Tramway Museum*

14 June 1958: Former Yellow service 7 (Bellahouston-Millerston – 9¾ miles, 52 minutes) replaced by trolleybuses. It was operated from Govan, Dennistoun (and latterly Dalmarnock) by Standards, Cunarders and, very briefly, Lightweights which following the closure were stored at Newlands whilst 1359-1392 were transferred to Dalmarnock which brought Cunarders regularly onto Argyle Street for the first time. Shipyard specials also ran from Shieldhall and Linthouse to Alexandra Park and Riddrie. **Track abandoned:** Bellahouston to Govan Road, Norfolk, Ballater, Abercromby and Bellgrove Streets. **Last cars:** 40 (Shieldhall-Riddrie); 141 (Shieldhall-Alexandra Park-Dennistoun depot); 143 (Millerston-Bellahouston-Govan depot); 338 (Riddrie-Bellahouston-Govan depot), 230 (Bellahouston-Riddrie-Dennistoun depot).

■ SERVICE PROFILE: 7

1381, Jura Street/Craigton Road, August 1957. *E.C. Bennett & Martin Jenkins/ Online Transport Archive*

Bellahouston, 1 February 1957. Note the triangular junction with Paisley Road West. After the line was extended in 1938 to serve the Empire Exhibition in nearby Bellahouston Park, thousands subsequently used the 7 to access the Park.
Hamish Stevenson/Online Transport Archive

668, Craigton Road, 7 July 1956. *John A. Clarke*

467, Elder Street/Langlands Road, 7 July 1956. *John A. Clarke*

133, Govan Road, 1958. This car is on a short-working to Riddrie. *Martin Jenkins collection*

6, Nelson Street, Tradeston, 1958. Note the SCWS headquarters in the background with the figure Light of Light adorning the dome. This car is working a shipyard special from the Govan area to Bridgeton Cross. *Hamish Stevenson/Online transport Archive*

300, Norfolk Street, 11 June 1958. *J.L. Stevenson*

71/497, Ballater Street, 11 June 1958. A busy scene in the heart of the Gorbals. *J.L. Stevenson*

465, Glasgow Green, April 1957. *E.C. Bennett & Martin Jenkins/Online Transport Archive*

257, James Street, Bridgeton, April 1957. In the background is the King's Cinema (1910-59), now a soft play and party centre. *W.D. McMillan/Travel Lens Photographic*

880, James Street, Bridgeton Cross, 28 May 1958. Cars on the 7 encountered many right angle bends but this car is at right angles to the track! Specials from this densely populated area ran from here to Hogganfield Loch and Millerston on Sunday afternoons. *G.W. Price collection*

272, Abercromby Street/Gallowgate, 28 July 1955. The 7 was known as 'The Glory Road' or 'The Yellow Peril' by the hard-working crews due to its heavy loadings in both directions during most of the day. *R.J.S. Wiseman/National Tramway Museum*

147, Cumbernauld Road, Onslow Drive, 19 July 1954. *R.J.S. Wiseman/National Tramway Museum*

1324, Cumbernauld Road/Gartloch Road, 17 April 1955. Nearby Hogganfield Loch attracted people from all over the city on warm days. *R.J.S. Wiseman/National Tramway Museum*

Cumbernauld Road, Hogganfield Loch. On the rural stretch near Millerston. *M.J. Lea/LRTA (London Area)/Online Transport Archive*

6 September 1958: Former blue service 4 (Hillington Road-George V Bridge-Springburn – 8¾ miles, 52 minutes) replaced. Operated from Govan and Possilpark by a mix of Standards and Cunarders, like the 27, this service linked industrial Springburn to the south side shipyards. After this closure, specials on the 12 were the only trams still using the fascinating section from Govan to Shieldhall where it was possible to see various standard gauge locomotives either operating along or cutting across the tram tracks. **Track abandoned:** Hillington Road to Shieldhall; Govan Road between Lorne Street and Paisley Road Toll. **Last car:** 1349 (Springburn-Hillington Road-Govan depot).

■ SERVICE PROFILE: 4

10/45/1001, Hillington Road, 6 April 1958. This was probably the last time one of the unloved Lightweights carried passengers, albeit enthusiasts on an organised tour. This section dated from 1926 when new tracks were laid skirting the site of George V Dock opened in 1931. Car 10 can be seen on page 57 at Baillieston making its final journey to the scrapyard. *Paul de Beer/Online Transport Archive*

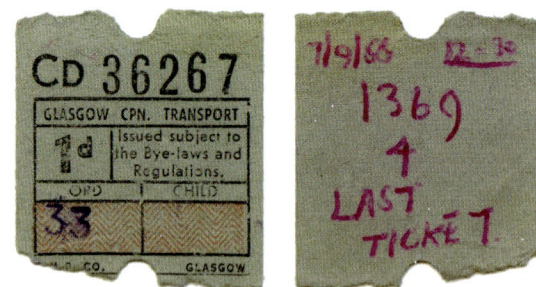

403, Renfrew Road, 10 September 1954. Due to flooding, the track level here was raised. Shortly afterwards a roundabout, dissected by track, was also built at the junction with Shieldhall Road in the background. *R.J.S. Wiseman/National Tramway Museum*

461, Renfrew Road, 6 July 1956. Note the large dockside crane in the background.
John A. Clarke

Renfrew Road, Linthouse, April 1957. This ex-colliery 0-4-0 built by Andrew Barclay in 1924 and owned by Alexander Stephen & Sons is seen at the entrance to their shipyard. *John Cadisch/Online Transport Archive*

EL.1, Renfrew Road, 6 July 1956. Also owned by Stephen's, this four-wheel battery electric loco is about to enter the shipyard after its 500 yard journey from Shieldhall Goods Yard. Built in 1919, it was scrapped in 1959. *John A. Clarke*

174, Govan Road, 23 June 1958. Following closure of service 7, the junction with Golspie Street was removed. Slightly heavier rail was used on this section to allow operation of trains between Fairfield Shipbuilding & Engineering yard and Govan Goods Yard exchange sidings. *John A. Clarke*

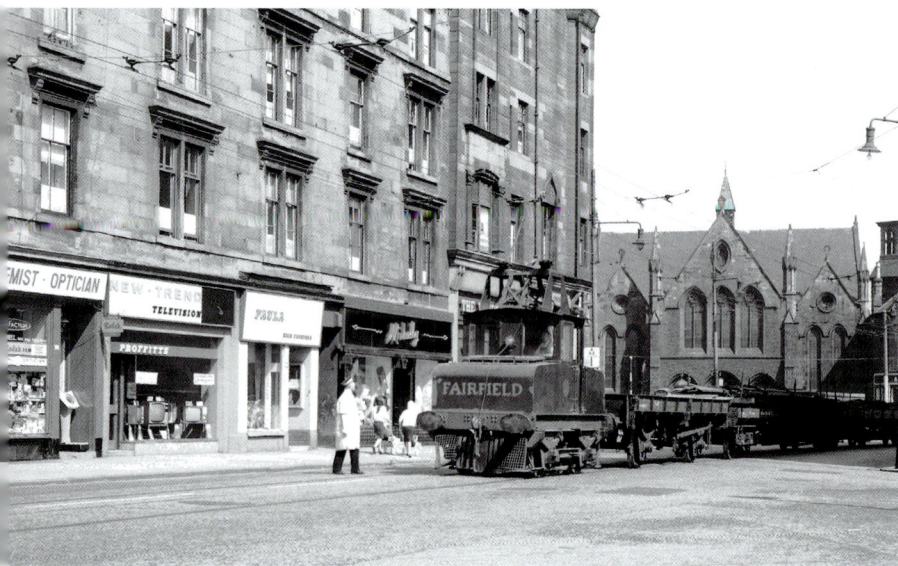

Govan Road, 27 May 1957. Fairfield's four-wheel steeple cab was built by English Electric in 1940. Here, it hauls a rake of wagons along the tram track between Fairfield's and the BR goods yard, a journey of some 600 yards. Note the cow-catcher and the small tower supporting the bow collector. After the trams finished, two trolleypoles were fitted which allowed the loco to draw power from its own pair of matching trolleybus-type wires until September 1966. *Struan Robertson/Online Transport Archive*

1107, Govan Road. This four-wheel battery electric loco built by English Electric in 1936 was used to transfer materials from Govan Goods Yard into the Harland & Wolff complex by means of a single track crossing with the tramway. *A.D. Packer*

191, Govan Road, 23 June 1958. Note the cranes in Harland & Wolff's Govan Shipyard and Clyde Foundry. *John A. Clarke*

1378, Govan Road. A vibrant scene with dockers, lorries, cranes and a crew change close to Govan depot. *Bob Docherty collection/Online Transport Archive*

137, Govan Road, Prince's Dock East, 23 June 1958. *John A. Clarke*

301, Paisley Road Toll, 23 June 1958. Note the intricate web of tram and trolleybus overhead at this major transport hub as well as the shelter, clock and Imperial cinema on the right. *John A. Clarke*

238, Keppochhill Road/Vere Street, 27 June 1958. *John A. Clarke*

16, Keppochhill Road/Carlisle Street, 27 June 1958. *John A. Clarke*

14 November 1958: Some fifteen shipyard specials operated for the last time during this Friday evening peak on service 12 (Shieldhall or Linthouse-Mount Florida – 6¼ miles/5½ miles, 33/29 minutes). **Track** abandoned: Shieldhall to Lorne Street. **Last car:** 373 (Shieldhall-Mount Florida).

SECTION PROFILE: SHIELDHALL-LORNE STREET, GOVAN

Left: **29, Bogmoor Road, 1 March 1958.** At peak times, this siding hosted several shipyard specials. *W.A.C. Smith/Transport Library*

Above: **13. Holmfauld Road, April 1957.** Sporting three crossovers, this siding catered for nearby labour-intensive shipyards and associated industrial premises. Latterly, construction of the under-river Whiteinch tunnel meant only the southern crossover could be used. *E.C. Bennett & Martin Jenkins/Online Transport Archive*

Below left: **416, Govan Road.** Cranes and ships are visible in the adjacent docks. *G.W. Price collection*

Below right: **779, Lorne Street, 23 June 1958.** Note that the track on Govan Road has already gone. This Standard was later preserved. *John A. Clarke*

15 November 1958: Another massive cull included the loss of former yellow service 12 (Paisley Road Toll-Mount Florida – 2¾ miles, 16 minutes). This was the last tram to trolleybus conversion in the UK and the last route not entering the central area. Owing to several sharp radius curves, only Standards were used, latterly from Govan depot. **Track abandoned:** entire route. **Last car:** 373 (Mount Florida-Govan depot).

SERVICE PROFILE: 12

16, Paisley Road Toll, 1958. Workers from the nearby docks, shipyards, railway yards, warehouses and factories form an orderly queue. Cars terminating here used a facing, as opposed to a trailing, crossover. *Charles Billette*

23, Milnpark Street, 7 July 1956. *John A. Clarke*

727, Seaward Street, 7 July 1956. Note Kinning Park sub-station on the right. *John A. Clarke*

393, Scotland Street, 17 June 1954. Part of the Kinning Park United Free Church (demolished) can be seen. *R.J.S. Wiseman/National Tramway Museum*

409, Shields Road, 1958. This stretch was noted for its ornate centre poles.
W.D. McMillan/Travel Lens Photographic

47, Nithsdale Road, Strathbungo station, April 1957. *John Cadisch/Online Transport Archive*

862, Shields Road. Rich in tramscapes, the 12 featured this very steep hill, at the foot of which was Howden Engineering. *E.C. Bennett & Martin Jenkins/Online Transport Archive*

986, Shields Road/Nithsdale Road, 7 July 1956. This Gloucester-built car survived until March 1958. The towering Pollokshaws West United Free Church survives as a children's nursery. *John A. Clarke*

416, Nithsdale Road/Nithsdale Street junction. Note the elegantly curved tenement building. *Hamish Stevenson/Online Transport Archive*

994, Allison Street/Cathcart Road, April 1957. The former Govanhill Church of Scotland was demolished in 1975. *E.C. Bennett & Martin Jenkins/Online Transport Archive*

207, Cathcart Road, September 1958. Latterly, cars rocked and swayed alarmingly on the badly worn, heavily corrugated track. *E.C. Bennett & Martin Jenkins/Online Transport Archive*

617, Mount Florida. This former white car bringing up the rear of a line of football trams was withdrawn in August 1958. *Hamish Stevenson/Online Transport Archive*

There was no direct replacement for former red service 17 (Anniesland to Farme Cross – 6¾ miles), which was operated from Dalmarnock and Partick by Standards, Coronations (from 1956) and Cunarders (from 1958). **Track abandoned:** Crow Road with depot workings on services 1 and 30 being re-routed. **Last Car:** 255 (Farme Cross-Dalmarnock depot).

■ SERVICE PROFILE: 17

Above left: **1376, Jordanhill Station, 20 October 1958.** This car was destroyed in the Dalmarnock depot fire of March 1961. *G.W. Price collection*

Above right: **334, Crow Road, 24 October 1958.** The car has just turned off Dumbarton Road and is tackling the long climb to Anniesland. This Standard was rebuilt in 1946 and withdrawn in November 1959. *G.W. Price collection*

Left: **444, Crow Road, 4 August 1955.** Seen passing the entrance to Partick Mineral Depot. The Kilmarnock bogie in the background, 1119, was probably on a brake-test run from Partick depot. *R.J.S. Wiseman/National Tramway Museum*

21, Argyle Street/Radnor Street, 24 June 1958. *John A. Clarke*

352, Argyle Street/Stobcross Street junction/Anderston Cross, 7 August 1954. *R.B. Parr/Scottish Tramway & Transport Society*

639, Bridgeton Cross, 9 August 1953. Note the complex track layout. *R.B. Parr/Scottish Tramway & Transport Society*

888, Dalmarnock Road/Cambuslang Road, 28 August 1958. *T.A. Packwood/Online Transport Archive*

Operated from Dalmarnock and Partick by Standards, Kilmarnock bogies, Coronations and, latterly, Cunarders, uni-directional service 26A (Clydebank or Scotstoun to Shawfield) was discontinued and service 26 was reorganised to serve both Farme Cross and Burnside. **Track abandoned:** none. **Last car:** not known.

SERVICE PROFILE: 26A

Left: 668, Clydebank, 30 November 1957. *Hamish Stevenson/Online Transport Archive*

Right: 1134, Scotstoun, 1957. *R.W.A. Jones/Online Transport Archive*

Below left: 145, Argyle Street/Sauchiehall Street, 24 June 1958. *John A Clark*

Below right: 1135, Bridgeton Cross, 1958. *Hamish Stevenson/Online Transport Archive*

16 November 1958: Heavily-used cross-city services 22 (Crookston-Lambhill – 7¾ miles, 49 minutes) and 32 (Crookston-Bishopbriggs – 8 miles, 48 minutes) replaced by buses. Latterly, they shared common trackage from Crookston to Tradeston where the 22 turned north over George V Bridge to Lambhill whilst the 32 headed north by way of Glasgow Bridge to Bishopbriggs. Operated from Govan and Possilpark depots, they were worked latterly by Standards and Cunarders. **Track abandoned:** Crookston to Lorne Street, Commerce Street, George V Bridge, Oswald Street. **Last Cars:** 447 (Lambhill-Crookston-Govan depot); 217 (Crookston-Lambhill-Possilpark depot); 178 (Crookston-Bishopbriggs-Possilpark depot); 288 (Crookston-Govan depot); 1171 last over George V Bridge, a late-night car returning to Newlands as an 8 using Kingston Street to access Bridge Street.

SERVICE PROFILES: 22, 32

Above left: **Crookston, August 1958.** *E.C. Bennett & Martin Jenkins/Online Transport Archive*

Above right: **Paisley Road West, approaching Crookston terminal stub, April 1957.** Note the warning sign on the left. *John Cadisch/Online Transport Archive*

Left: **Paisley Road West, April 1957.** The Vogue cinema was demolished in 1963. *John Cadisch/Online Transport Archive*

394, Paisley Road West, 23 June 1958. The Westway cinema closed in 1959 but survived in various guises until demolished in 2003. *John A. Clarke*

1355/661, Paisley Road West/Corkerhill Road, 30 July 1955. *R.J.S. Wiseman/National Tramway Museum*

1366, Paisley Road West, August 1957. The Greyhound (later Speedway) Stadium was demolished in 1972. *E.C. Bennett & Martin Jenkins/Online Transport Archive*

358, Paisley Road West, Ibrox station bridge, 17 July 1954. Also on view are a tar boiler, semaphore signals and the tracks into Broomloan Road. *R.J.S. Wiseman/National Tramway Museum*

549/574, Paisley Road West, Ibrox Church, August 1957. *E.C. Bennett & Martin Jenkins/ Online Transport Archive*

1363, Paisley Road, 1958. Crossing bridge over freight line to the docks. *Roy Hamilton/ Online Transport Archive*

1358, Paisley Road West/Lambhill Street, 23 June 1958. *John A. Clarke*

1385, Nelson Street, Tradeston, 1956. *Frank Hunt/LRTA (London Area)/Online Transport Archive*

108, Oswald Street, 1958. Having crossed George V Bridge, 22s headed north towards Lambhill. This car is seen earlier travelling south on service 4. Note the sign for the city zoo, the section box and the coil of wire at the top of the traction pole. *W.D. McMillan/Travel Lens Photographic*

471, Hope Street, 24 June 1958. Scotland's oldest theatre, the Theatre Royal, was occupied by Scottish Television (STV) from 1957 to 1975. It is now an entertainment and conference centre. *John A. Clarke*

269, Garscube Road, 24 June 1958. *John A. Clarke*

316, Round Toll, 24 June 1958. Note the Astoria in the background. Renowned as 'the largest working class cinema in Scotland', it served in this capacity from 1931 until 1962. The building was demolished in 1995. *John A. Clarke*

157, Possil Road aqueduct carrying the Forth & Clyde Canal, 27 June 1958. *John A. Clarke*

129, Balmore Road/Possil Station, 26 June 1958. *T.A. Packwood/Online Transport Archive*

125, Balmore Road, 1958. *W.D. McMillan/Travel Lens Photographic*

779, Lambhill, Easter 1958. Note the terminus cafe. This car is preserved. *Paul de Beer/ Online Transport Archive*

54, Nelson Street/Bridge Street, 23 June 1958. After crossing under the approach to Glasgow Central, the 32s turned towards Glasgow Bridge for the run to Bishopbriggs. *John A. Clarke*

374, Sauchiehall Street/Renfield Street. *G.W. Price collection*

244, Springburn Road, August 1957. *E.C. Bennett & Martin Jenkins/Online Transport Archive*

155, Kirkintilloch Road/Stuart Drive, 26 June 1958. *John A. Clarke*

Although retained to house vehicles awaiting scrap, Govan depot closed to service cars on 15 November 1958. Dating from 1915, it had capacity for 128 trams on 14 tracks. Also closed was the Clothing Store and Sand Drying shed on nearby Admiral Street.

Above: **Part of the main depot area, August 1958.** *John Cadisch/Online Transport Archive*

Right: **462, depot entrance, 25 May 1958.** A fitter walks across, as a motorwoman drives past other colleagues. The car was withdrawn within days of this picture being taken. *Hamish Stevenson/Online Transport Archive*

Below left: **1369, Brand Street, September 1958.** Note the spark from the bow as it passes under newly erected trolleybus overhead. This car was lost in the Dalmarnock depot fire of March 1961. *E.C. Bennett & Martin Jenkins/Online Transport Archive*

Below right: **No. 39, Admiral Street, 1957.** The sand-drier plant is visible in the background. *A.D. Packer*

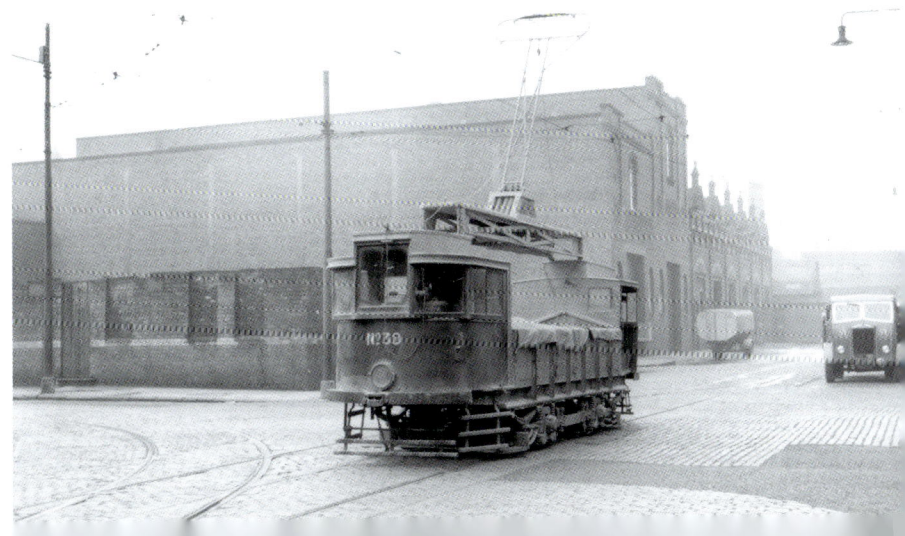

GLASGOW
CORPORATION
TRAMWAYS
1 JANUARY 1959

Some peak hour services, shipyard
specials and other extras not shown

N
W E
S

Depots	
Dk	Dalmarnock
De	Dennistoun
G	Govan
M	Maryhill
N	Newlands
Ph	Parkhead
Pk	Partick
Pp	Possilpark
Other facilities	
CW	Coplawhill Works

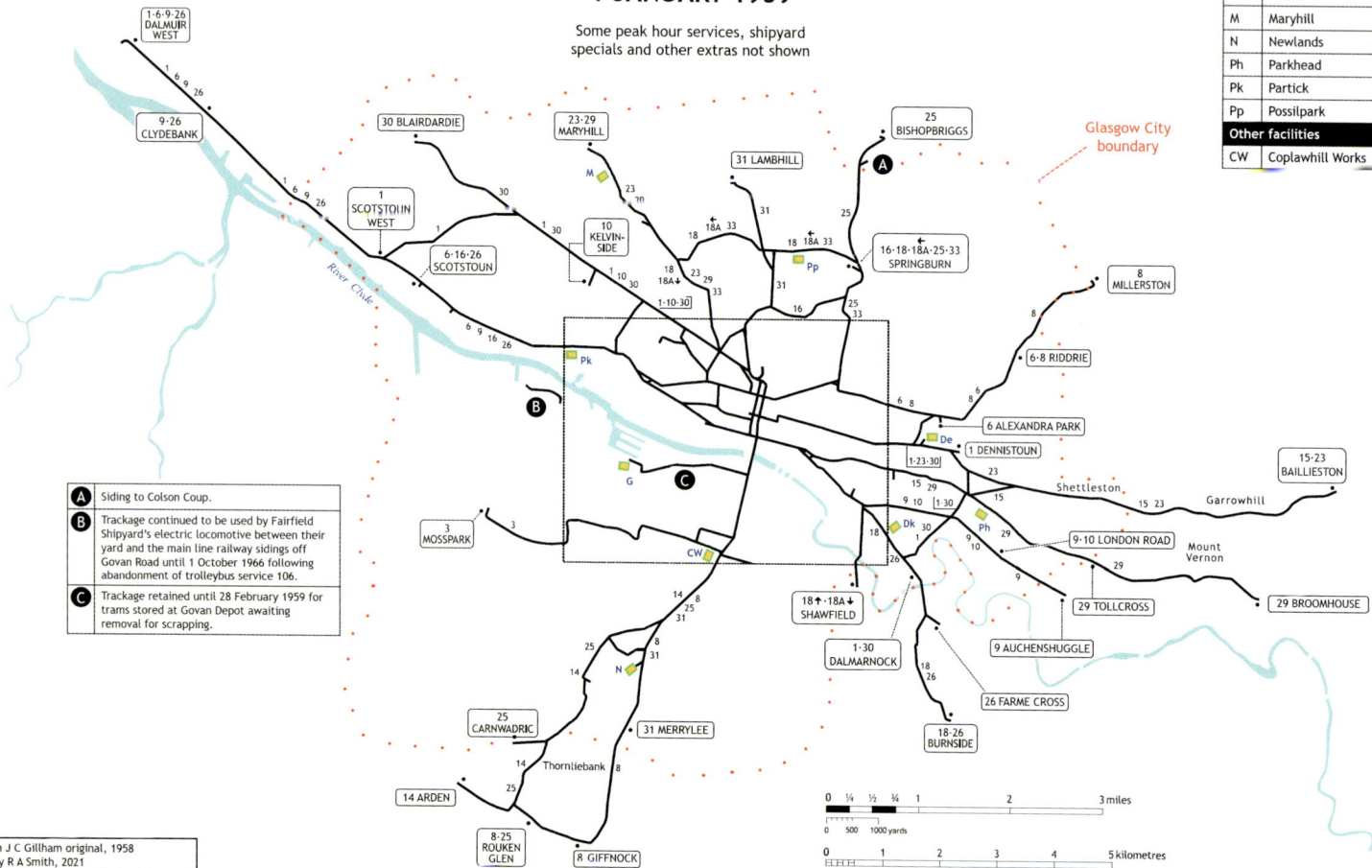

Glasgow City
boundary

River Clyde

1·6·9·26
DALMUIR
WEST

9·26
CLYDEBANK

30 BLAIRDARDIE

23·29
MARYHILL

31 LAMBHILL

25
BISHOPBRIGGS

A

M

1
SCOTSTOUN
WEST

6·16·26
SCOTSTOUN

10
KELVIN-
SIDE

Pp

16·18·18A·25·33
SPRINGBURN

8
MILLERSTON

Pk

6·8 RIDDRIE

B

De

6 ALEXANDRA PARK

1 DENNISTOUN

15·23
BAILLIESTON

G

Shettleston

Garrowhill

C

Dk

Ph

9·10 LONDON ROAD

Mount
Vernon

3
MOSSPARK

CW

29 TOLLCROSS

29 BROOMHOUSE

14
ARDEN

18↑·18A↓
SHAWFIELD

9 AUCHENSHUGGLE

1·30
DALMARNOCK

26 FARME CROSS

25
CARNWADRIC

N

31 MERRYLEE

18·26
BURNSIDE

Thornliebank

14 ARDEN

8·25
ROUKEN
GLEN

8 GIFFNOCK

A Siding to Colson Coup.

B Trackage continued to be used by Fairfield
Shipyard's electric locomotive between their
yard and the main line railway sidings off
Govan Road until 1 October 1966 following
abandonment of trolleybus service 106.

C Trackage retained until 28 February 1959 for
trams stored at Govan Depot awaiting
removal for scrapping.

0 ¼ ½ ¾ 1 2 3 miles
0 500 1000 yards
0 1 2 3 4 5 kilometres

Based on J C Gillham original, 1958
Drawn by R A Smith, 2021
Adapted for this volume by Charles Roberts

1959

During the year, all but one of the south side services using Glasgow Bridge were abandoned together with the lines to Lambhill, Bishopbriggs and Millerston. More Standards and ex-Liverpool cars withdrawn and badly-damaged modern cars stopped being repaired. Peak demand on 31 May was for 443 trams to operate the 130½ miles of track.

3 January 1959: The need to replace a bridge over the River Kelvin led to the premature closure of the short University branch. Service 3 diverted to terminate at nearby Park Road and service 14 at Kelvingrove (Radnor Street). **Track abandoned:** University Avenue, Gibson Street, Eldon Street. **Last car:** 1324 (University-Newlands depot**).**

SECTION PROFILE: UNIVERSITY BRANCH

Above left: **1324, University, 1958.** This car was destroyed in the Dalmarnock depot fire of March 1961. *Martin Jenkins collection/Online Transport Archive*

Above middle: **311, Kelvin Way/Gibson Street, 3 August 1955.** *R.J.S. Wiseman/National Tramway Museum*

Above right: **1393, Eldon Street/Woodlands Road, 24 June 1958.** Another Dalmarnock fire victim. *John A. Clarke*

Left: **139, Eldon Street, 24 June 1958.** The ornate, but weak, bridge can be seen in the foreground. *John A. Clarke*

28 February 1959: Govan depot closed having been cleared of cars awaiting scrap. **Track abandoned:** Lorne Street to Nelson Street/Bridge Street junction.

14 March 1959: Last day for former red service 8 (Millerston-Giffnock – 10¼ miles, 58 minutes). This heavily-used cross-city route was interworked with service 25 to form a circle at the south end. Latterly, the 8/25 combination was operated from Possilpark, Dennistoun and Newlands depots by Standards, Coronations, and Cunarders. **Track abandoned:** Millerston to Riddrie and Merrylee to Giffnock (Milverton Road). Service 25 extended along Rouken Glen Road to Milverton Road crossover. **Last car:** 270 (officially Giffnock-Riddrie but driver persuaded to continue to Millerston before returning to Dennistoun depot).

■ SERVICE PROFILE: 8

Above left: 1302, Station Road, Millerston, April 1957. *John Cadisch/Online Transport Archive*

Left: 434, Cumbernauld Road/Hogganfield Loch, 7 August 1953. *R.J.S. Wiseman/National Tramway Museum*

Above right: 13, Smithycroft Road, 1957. Note the bridge over the Monkland Canal. *W.D. McMillan/Travel Lens Photographic*

1236, Smithycroft Road, 10 August 1955. For many years, this track was shared with services 6 and 7. *R.J.S. Wiseman/National Tramway Museum*

1149, Cumbernauld Road, September 1958. The Vogue cinema (1938-68) is now a Grade B listed building. *E.C. Bennett & Martin Jenkins/Online Transport Archive*

1258, Alexandra Parade, 27 June 1958. The imposing Wills cigar and cigarette factory (1952) is now the City Park Business Centre. *John A. Clarke*

156, Townhead, 1958. *W.D. McMillan/Travel Lens Photographic*

1310/685, Jamaica Street, May 1955. *Ray DeGroote/Online Transport Archive*

1304, Bridge Street/Norfolk Street, 23 June 1958. *John A. Clarke*

88, Kilmarnock Road, 25 June 1958. Note the crossover where cars from Old Pollokshaws (see page 126) reversed in order to reach Newlands depot. *John A. Clarke*

1003, Kilmarnock Road/near approach road to Newlands depot, 15 June 1950. Crews disliked this Lightweight owing to its cramped cab. *Nigel McMillan*

Above: **Fenwick Road/Merryton Avenue, April 1957.** *John Cadisch/Online Transport Archive*

Below: **Fenwick Road, Giffnock,** The Tudor cinema (1936) was demolished after it closed in 1962. *Nigel McMillan collection*

1250, Rouken Glen Road/Milverton Road, 7 September 1958. Although some 8s reversed here, the majority continued on as 25s towards Thornliebank whilst most 25s arriving at Rouken Glen returned north as 8s. With replacement of the 8, the track seen here stretching towards Eastwood Toll was abandoned as far as Merrylee. However, the crossover was now used by 25s which were extended to this point. *Hamish Stevenson/ Online Transport Archive*

2 May 1959: Springburn circular service 33 (6½ miles, 40 minutes) discontinued on economic grounds. Operated from Maryhill and Possilpark depots, this was a Standard stronghold until Coronations appeared during the final months. The circle worked both ways from Springburn – clockwise via Springburn Road, Parliamentary Road, Sauchiehall Street, Maryhill Road and Bilsland Drive and anti-clockwise in the reverse order. **Track abandoned:** none. **Last car:** not known.

SERVICE PROFILE: 33

306, Springburn Road, 27 April 1958. Latterly, 33s were poorly patronised outside peak times. *G.W. Price collection*

642/246, Parliamentary Road/Monkland Street, 26 June 1958. *John A. Clarke*

124, St George's Cross, 24 June 1958. *John A. Clarke*

1286, Bilsland Drive, 29 April 1959. Rare view of a Coronation on this service. *J.L. Stevenson*

469, Bilsland Drive, 2 May 1959. *Hamish Stevenson/Online Transport Archive*

522, Hawthorn Street, 29 April 1959. *J.L. Stevenson collection*

862, Hawthorn Street, 2 May 1959. This former yellow car was nearly 60 years old when withdrawn in the September. *Hamish Stevenson/Online Transport Archive*

1005, Springburn, 1947. When new, 1005 was entrusted to selected drivers when first assigned to Possilpark depot to work the 33. *R R Clark/Scottish Tramway & Transport Society*

2 May 1959: Driver training school closed. After learning the ropes by driving ex-Paisley District 1017 up and down Coplaw Street, new recruits were then usually given an ex-Works Standard to prepare them for the road ahead. **Track abandoned:** Coplaw Street. 1017 became a shunter at the Works.

1017, Coplaw Street, April 1958. It is said that the Chief of the Motor School in the 1920s deliberately specified a short bow tower so 1017 could not be purloined for use on the Duntocher route if there was a shortage of 'wee caurs'. The Royal Samaritan Hospital closed in 1961 is now flats. *E.C. Bennett & Martin Jenkins/Online Transport Archive*

370, Coplaw Street, September 1958. Displaying an 'L' board, the car is at the limit of the training track. Note the knot of trainees and the old style rail with shallow grooves hence the need for recently overhauled cars with high tyres. This former red car, scrapped in November 1960, was the last Round Dash Standard to receive a yearly overhaul. *E.C. Bennett & Martin Jenkins/Online Transport Archive*

Pollokshaws Road, 25 June 1958. Carrying a 'L' board, this Cunarder was spotted near Shawlands Cross. *John A. Clarke*

1017, Mosspark Boulevard, 23 February 1958. This was probably the only occasion a non-passenger car was used for an enthusiasts' tour. 1017 is now preserved. *Hamish Stevenson/Online Transport Archive*

5 June 1959: Alexandra Park-Springburn-Kelvingrove 'specials' withdrawn. **Last Car:** 232

6 June 1959: Service 25 (Bishopbriggs to Carnwadric – 7½ miles, 47 minutes, or Rouken Glen – 9¼ miles, 55 minutes) replaced by buses. Worked by Standards, Coronations and Cunarders from Dennistoun (until March 1959), Newlands and Possilpark depots, this was another long north-south route serving a mix of residential suburbs, industrial neighbourhoods and major inner-city streets. **Track abandoned:** Bishopbriggs to Springburn; Carnwadric branch and all of Rouken Glen Road. **Last car:** 260 (Bishopbriggs-Possilpark depot).

SERVICE PROFILE: 25

Above left: **70, Bishopbriggs, 1958.** *Ian Dunnet/Online Transport Archive*

Above right: **9, Kirkintilloch Road/Colston Road, 1957.** *W.D. McMillan/ Travel Lens Photographic*

Left: **403, Springburn Road North, 1 September 1954.** Two Albion tower wagons deal with an overhead wire problem. *R.J.S. Wiseman/National Tramway Museum*

50, Springburn Road, 1958. Note Elmvale Street siding on the left and the coaling stage at Eastfield engine shed in the far distance. *W.D. McMillan/Travel Lens Photographic*

1214, Springburn Road, 26 June 1958. Note that both tracks are offset to the right of the road as well as the poor state of the surface. This was one of many cars lost in the Dalmarnock depot fire of March 1961. *John A. Clarke*

427, Castle Street/Royston Road, 13 September 1954. This former red Standard is cresting the bridge over the canal serving St Rollox basin. This area has all but disappeared. *R.J.S. Wiseman/National Tramway Museum*

579/681, Parliamentary Road/Monkland Street, 14 September 1954. Trouble at Townhead. This is another area which is unrecognisable today. *R.J.S. Wiseman/National Tramway Museum*

Above: 1338, Parliamentary Road/North Frederick Street, 26 June 1958. *John A. Clarke*

Left: 234, Parliamentary Road, 6 June 1959. *Hamish Stevenson/Online Transport Archive*

Below left: 300, Renfield Street, May 1951. *W.J. Wyse/LRTA (London Area)/Online Transport Archive*

Below right: 672, Eglinton Toll, 11 September 1954. Concerned staff congregate round this damaged car which was fortunately near to the Works. *R.J.S. Wiseman/National Tramway Museum*

Shawlands Cross, 1958. The Coronation on the left has just left Newlands depot and will soon take up service on the 3. *W.D. McMillan/Travel Lens Photographic*

1330, Nether Auldhouse Road, 1958. *W.D. McMillan/Travel Lens Photographic*

1255, Thornliebank Road, 25 June 1958. This car had the last replacement Coronation body built at Coplawhill. *John A. Clarke*

165, Carnwadric, June 1957. *Marcus Eavis/Online Transport Archive*

Boydstone Road, April 1958. *John Cadisch/Online Transport Archive*

1302, Rouken Glen Road/Rowallan Road, April 1958 *E.C. Bennett & Martin Jenkins/Online Transport Archive*

Possilpark depot closed to trams. Accessed from Hawthorn Street, it had 20 tracks for 133 cars.

Above: **Depot entrance, 1958.** Due to its tight internal curves, only Standards were based here after 1941. *W.D. McMillan/Travel Lens Photographic*

Right: **190, interior, 2 May 1959.** This view shows some of the pits and wooden cleaning galleries. *Hamish Stevenson/Online Transport Archive*

6 September 1959: Service 16 curtailed at the east end of Keppochhill Road. **Track abandoned:** Springburn Road between Elmvale Street and Keppochhill Road. **Last car:** 1179.

SECTION PROFILE: SPRINGBURN ROAD

155/214, Elmvale Street, April 1957. *Marcus Eavis/Online Transport Archive*

Springburn Road, September 1958. *E.C. Bennett & Martin Jenkins/Online Transport Archive*

7 September 1959: Dalmuir Canal Swing Bridge closed to trams at 9am to allow for urgent repairs. All cars now reverse at Dalmuir. Specials on services 1 and 6 discontinued before the bridge reopened.

874, Dalmuir West, September 1958. This former yellow car was nearly 60 years old when scrapped. *E.C. Bennett & Martin Jenkins/Online Transport Archive*

Canal bridge, 1953. *R.W.A. Jones/Online Transport Archive*

30 October 1959: The 1½ mile eastern limit of former blue service 6 between Riddrie and Alexandra Park operated for the last time. **Track abandoned:** Smithycroft Road and part of Cumbernauld Road. Shipyard workings to Whiteinch and Dalmuir discontinued. **Last car from Riddrie:** 1143.

SECTION PROFILE: RIDDRIE-ALEXANDRA PARK

Above left: **1212, Smithycroft Road, 22 August 1959.** Barlinnie prison can be seen in the background.

Above right: **1168, Cumbernauld Road, 22 August 1959.** Note the short loading island on the inbound track only and side bracket arms supporting the new trolleybus overhead.

Left: **1212, Cumbernauld Road/Edinburgh Road, 22 August 1959.** The Rex cinema (1931-73) is no longer standing.
E.C. Bennett & Martin Jenkins/Online Transport Archive (all)

31 October 1959: Remainder of service 6 (Alexandra Park to Scotstoun – 6¼ miles, 38 minutes) replaced by buses. Worked from Dennistoun and Partick by Standards, Coronations and Cunarders (last few months), it served a mix of dockland, residential and industrial neighbourhoods. **Track abandoned:** everything east of Renfield Street; depot link along Cumbernauld Road. **Last cars:** 1206 (Scotstoun-Alexandra Park-Dennistoun depot); 1153 (Alexandra Park-Partick depot).

■ SERVICE PROFILE: 6

Above left: **1218, Aitken Street, Alexandra Park stub terminus, September 1959.** This car was lost in the Dalmarnock depot conflagration in March 1961. *E.C. Bennett & Martin Jenkins/Online Transport Archive*

Above right: **Alexandra Parade, September 1958.** *E.C. Bennett & Martin Jenkins/ Online Transport Archive*

Below: **Cumbernauld Road, 22 August 1959.** Depot only section for workings to and from Dennistoun. *E.C. Bennett & Martin Jenkins/Online Transport Archive*

Right: **61/1248, Parliamentary Road, 6 June 1959.** *Hamish Stevenson/Online Transport Archive*

1144, Charing Cross, 24 June 1958. *John A. Clarke*

219, Sauchiehall Street, 1958. *W.D. McMillan/Travel Lens Photographic*

47, Sauchiehall Street/Radnor Street, 24 June 1958. The latter had been terminus for the 14 since January. *John A. Clarke*

370/113, Dumbarton Road turning into Balmoral Street terminal stub, September 1958. *E.C. Bennett & Martin Jenkins/Online Transport Archive*

Former blue service 14 (Kelvingrove-Arden – 6½ miles, 45 minutes) replaced by buses. Operated from Newlands depot by Standards, Coronations and Cunarders, it mostly served residential suburbs on the south side. **Track abandoned:** Radnor Street, west end of Sauchiehall Street, Pollokshaws/ Thornliebank/Boydstone and Nitshill Roads. **Last car:** 1398 (Kelvingrove-Arden-Newlands depot).

SERVICE PROFILE: 14

Above left: **992, Sauchiehall Street, 24 June 1958.** This section of Sauchiehall Street was also used by cars returning to Partick depot. This Standard was photographed after the morning peak. *John A. Clarke*

Above right: **629, Renfield Street, 10 August 1954.** *R.J.S. Wiseman/National Tramway Museum*

Left: **665, Jamaica Street, 1959.** Surviving until November 1960, this was the last of a batch of Hex-Dash Standards built in 1923/24. *Marcus Eavis/ Online Transport Archive*

Eglinton Toll, September 1959.

1219, Pollokshaws Road/Albert Drive, August 1959.

63, Pollokshaws Road, August 1959.

234, Pollokshaws Road/Minard Road, August 1959. *E.C. Bennett & Martin Jenkins/ Online Transport Archive (all)*

413, Shawlands Cross, 30 October 1959. *Hamish Stevenson/Online Transport Archive*

63, Pollokshaws Road, approaching Shawlands Cross, 25 June 1958. *John A. Clarke*

Nether Auldhouse Road, September 1958. A few specials used this siding at peak hours. *E.C. Bennett & Martin Jenkins/Online Transport Archive*

1322, Harriet Street/Thornliebank Road, August 1959. *E.C. Bennett & Martin Jenkins/Online Transport Archive*

1322, Thornliebank Road, August 1959. Repairs to the setts surrounding the track involved the use of a tar boiler.

1217, Thornliebank Station, September 1958. Until June, this had been the junction for the Carnwadric branch.

1040, Thornliebank. August 1959.

35, Spiersbridge, September 1958. The quarter mile from here to Arden was the last remnant of the former Paisley District system. Until early April 1949, this crossover was used by cars terminating here on services 14 and 28 (see page 20). *E.C. Bennett & Martin Jenkins/Online Transport Archive (all)*

The depot connection track through Old Pollokshaws was also closed. **Track abandoned:** Greenview Street, Pleasance Street, Coustonholm Road.

SECTION PROFILE: OLD POLLOKSHAWS

459, Pleasance Street, 5 May 1959. This narrow section, with its mix of single and double track and absence of coloured light signals, had an old-world atmosphere unlike any other part of the system, which has now all but disappeared. *J.L. Stevenson*

1331, Pleasance Street, August 1959. *E.C. Bennett & Martin Jenkins/Online Transport Archive*

Turning from Coustonholm Road into Pleasance Street, August 1959. Note former Pollokshaws depot in the background. *E.C. Bennett & Martin Jenkins/Online Transport Archive*

1213, Coustonholm Road, 10 August 1959. Between March and December 1959, any car returning from any point to Newlands depot had to show 31. *Garth Tilt*

5 December 1959: Service 31 (Lambhill-Merrylee – 5¾ miles, 45 minutes) withdrawn without replacement on economic grounds. Introduced in 1949, it was operated by Standards, Coronations and Cunarders from Newlands and Possilpark (until June 1959) depots. At one point, it had been earmarked as one of the last routes to operate. **Track abandoned:** Strachur Street, Balmore Road, Possil Road, Kilmarnock Road south of Newlands depot. Saracen Street retained until March 1961. **Last car:** 1258 (Lambhill-Newlands depot).

SERVICE PROFILE: 31

Above: **231, Balmore Road, 1958.** *W.D. McMillan/Travel Lens Photographic*

Right: **234, Balmore Road/Hawthorn Street, 28 November 1959.** The Vogue cinema closed in 1968 but has since been put to other uses. *Hamish Stevenson/Online Transport Archive*

Below left: **1327, Sauchiehall Street. Passing the Locarno.** *G.W. Morant/Online Transport Archive*

Below right: **306, Union Street/Argyle Street, May 1955.** The car is destined for Pollokshaws which was the southside terminus until moved to Merrylee in April 1956. *Ray DeGroote/Online Transport Archive*

83, Pollokshaws Road, Shawlands, August 1959. Note the horse and cart.
E.C. Bennett & Martin Jenkins/Online Transport Archive

1247, Pollokshaws Road/Marywood Square, August 1959. *E.C. Bennett & Martin Jenkins/ Online Transport Archive*

191, Kilmarnock Road/Coustonholm Road, 25 June 1958. The track in the foreground was part of the depot only track through Old Pollokshaws. *John A. Clarke*

502, Merrylee, 1958. The car is at the final 31 terminus which had been relocated here on safety grounds in August 1957. *W.D. McMillan/Travel Lens Photographic*

1960

This year witnessed significant losses including the final stretches of reserved track, passenger traffic over Glasgow Bridge, replacement of the last Standard only routes, withdrawal of the final 'Goddesses', as well as the closure of Parkhead and Newlands depots. At the beginning of March, the remaining routes were worked by some 400 cars of which about a quarter were Standards. By 31 May, 281 trams were in daily use although by December, the number of Standards and Kilmarnock bogies had dropped to around thirty . The track needed constant attention whilst staff shortages were an increasing problem and breakdowns and disruptions were all too common.

12 March 1960: Former green service 1 (Scotstoun West to Dennistoun or Dalmarnock – full journey, 8¾ miles, 55 minutes) and service 30 (Blairdardie, Knightswood or Anniesland to Dennistoun or Dalmarnock – full journey 8¼ miles, 55 minutes) replaced by buses. Sharing the same track east of Anniesland and worked jointly by up to 46 Standards from Partick, Dennistoun and Dalmarnock, these frequent, heavily-used routes served districts with varying levels of affluence and architecture. **Track abandoned:** Kingsway, Anniesland Road, Great Western Road (except between Hyndland Road and Park Road) and Carntyne Road. The section of Duke Street between Shettleston Road and Parkhead Cross was used occasionally until closure of Dennistoun depot. Works cars also continued running west from St George's Cross until track lifting work on the Great Western Road reservations was completed. **Last cars:** 121 (Last to short turn to Kelvinside), 126 (eastbound from Scotstoun West); 113 (to Scotstoun West); 9 (Blairdardie-Partick depot).

▊ SERVICE PROFILE: 1, 30

984, Clydebank, 24 March 1949. At certain times, service 1 operated to various points including Yoker, Dalmuir and Dalmuir West. This car was scrapped as early as October 1952. *Michael H. Waller/Online Transport Archive*

1309, Scotstoun West, 1959. Until the end, an occasional shipyard special into the city was sometimes worked in the evening by a Coronation or Cunarder. *Vic Goldberg/LCC Tramways Trust*

669, Anniesland Road/Kingsway, September 1958. *E.C. Bennett & Martin Jenkins/Online Transport Archive*

668, Anniesland Road, September 1958. The cottages on the right still survive. *E.C. Bennett & Martin Jenkins/Online Transport Archive*

1100, Anniesland Road/Great Western Road, March 1960. This one-off, rebuilt Kilmarnock bogie was usually to be found working specials on Dumbarton Road but sometimes it ventured to Anniesland to work an early morning special to Clydebank. 1100 last ran in service on 1 November 1961. *Brian Longworth/Online Transport Archive*

27, Great Western Road, 24 June 1958. The first of three views on the 1½ miles of reserved track between Blairdardie and Anniesland Cross. Overlooked by the Kilpatrick Hills the car is on the 1949 extension. *Marcus Eavis/Online Transport Archive*

102, Great Western Road, September 1958. Birrell's building, famous for 'Milady Chocolates', was demolished in the mid-1990s and Knightswood bus garage (far left) closed in 2004. *E.C. Bennett & Martin Jenkins/Online Transport Archive*

9, Great Western Road/Bingham's Pond, 4 September 1959. Remarkably, this Standard was repaired and had the dubious honour of being the very last tram to leave Blairdardie. Another accident occurred near here when a bus overturned in front of a tram, killing the motorman. *Straun Robertson/Online Transport Archive*

24, Great Western Road/Anniesland, August 1954. Opened as the *Ascot* in 1939, the cinema finally closed in 1975. Today, its facade forms part of a luxury flat development. *Phil Tatt/Online Transport Archive*

140, Great Western Road, August 1954. This view captures the undulating sweep of the city's longest and straightest road. This was a rare example of a paved reservation. *Phil Tatt/Online Transport Archive*

Above: 230, Great Western Road/Kelvinbridge (1891), 24 June 1958. Note the horse drawn cart. *John A. Clarke*

Left: 657, Great Western Road, 28 February 1959. Note the distinctive Botanic Gardens station, closed in 1939 and destroyed by fire in 1970. *Hamish Stevenson/Online Transport Archive*

Below left: 154, St George's Cross, 1957. *John Cadisch/Online Transport Archive*

Below right: 59, New City Road, 1959. *Charles Billette*

Above: **700, George Street, 1946**. This car was an early casualty, being scrapped in June 1952. *R.R. Clark/Scottish Tramway & Transport Society*

Right: **172, St Vincent Street, 19 September 1959**. Some cars short working into the city from the east end on services 1 and 30 used this siding. *Hamish Stevenson/Online Transport Archive*

Below left: **402, George Square, 1956**. *Joe and Richard Braun/Electric Railroaders' Association*

Below right: **190, George Street, September 1959**. This crossover was used by various specials terminating in the city, including shipyard specials from Clydebank working via service 1. *E.C. Bennett & Martin Jenkins/Online Transport Archive*

183, George Street, September 1958. *E.C. Bennett & Martin Jenkins/Online Transport Archive*

288, Duke Street/Cumbernauld Road, September 1958. *E.C. Bennett & Martin Jenkins/Online Transport Archive*

Carntyne Road, April 1958. Shown on screens as Dennistoun, this stub terminus had two crossovers and was overlooked by soot-encrusted tenements. *John Cadisch/Online Transport Archive*

Duke Street, 1959. Deep in the heart of the industrial east end was William Beardmore's Parkhead forge. Here, one of their locos No. 2, a diesel-electric 0-4-0 of 1959, crosses the road. *W.D. McMillan/Travel Lens Photographic*

116, Duke Street, Parkhead, 10 October 1959. This car is about to bite into the restricted curves which prevented the use of bogie cars. *Hamish Stevenson/Online Transport Archive*

168, Parkhead Cross, 9 January 1960. Schedules book in hand, a time-keeper oversees cars emerging from Springfield Road. *Hamish Stevenson/Online Transport Archive*

176, Springfield Road, 8 August 1953. Crowds of supporters make their way from the nearby Celtic FC ground. *R.J.S. Wiseman/National Tramway Museum*

Springfield Road, September 1958. Following replacement of the 1 and 30, this one mile section from Parkhead Cross to Dalmarnock Road was retained for depot workings. *E.C. Bennett & Martin Jenkins/Online Transport Archive*

Parkhead depot closed to trams on the same night as the 1 and 30. With capacity for 80 cars on nine tracks, it had, in recent times, housed Standards, Coronations and Green Goddesses. On closure, the Standards went to Dalmarnock and the Coronations to Dennistoun.

1030, part of the yard and depot area, September 1959. Prone to water ingress, some of the stylish curved windows on the ex-Liverpool cars had been replaced. This Goddess fell from grace the following February.

Cunarder, Parkhead depot. This defective car has been brought into the yard by a Coronation. In the background, a Goddess poses in the depot washing machine through which all cars had to pass. However, this was not used to wash the ex-Liverpool cars as their bodies were less than waterproof.

15 March 1960: pointsman's control tower at Parkhead Cross decommissioned.

1230, Westmuir Street, Parkhead Cross, September 1959. From the tower (right), the pointsman operated the electrically-powered points in order to keep cars moving through this complex junction with the minimum of delay. *E.C. Bennett & Martin Jenkins/ Online Transport Archive (all)*

4 June 1960: former blue service 10 (Kelvinside-London Road – 6 miles, 41 minutes) discontinued. Worked from Dalmarnock and Partick depots by Standards, Coronations and Cunarders (after June 1958) it basically provided extra capacity on the eastern leg of service 9. **Track abandoned:** Hyndland Road, Great Western Road. **Last car:** 1313 (London Road-Kelvinside-Partick depot).

■ SERVICE PROFILE: 10

Above left: **283, Kelvinside, 4 June 1960.** By now, most surviving Standards looked grubby and neglected. *E.C. Bennett & Martin Jenkins/Online Transport Archive*

Above right: **671, Hyndland Road/Great Western Road, 24 June 1958.** *John A. Clarke/Online Transport Archive*

Left: **234, Great Western Road, 4 June 1960.** Many elegant properties grace this part of the city. *A.S. Clayton/ Online Transport Archive*

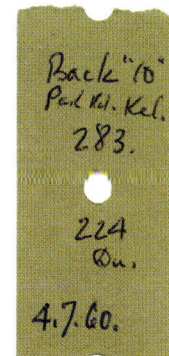

681/1398, Park Road, 4 June 1960. Having waited for the 3 to reverse, the 10 will now turn left onto Great Western Road. *E.C. Bennett & Martin Jenkins/Online Transport Archive*

1267, Elmbank Street/Bothwell Street, 1 April 1960. *John A. Clarke*

249, Hope Street/Argyle Street, 24 March 1959. Note the extremely crumpled number blind. *Hamish Stevenson/Online Transport Archive*

1189, Argyle Street, 1956. *W.J. Wyse collection/LRTA (London Area)/Online Transport Archive*

614, London Road, 30 August 1954. Note the goods train crossing the girder bridge.
R.J.S. Wiseman/National Tramway Museum

506, London Road, 5 September 1959. *Hamish Stevenson/Online Transport Archive*

London Road/Springfield Road, 1959. *John Cadisch/Online Transport Archive*

1095, London Road, June 1959. A Cunarder is reversing in the background.
A.S. Clayton/Online Transport Archive

4 June 1960: Former white service 3 (Park Road-Mosspark – 6 miles, 37 minutes) replaced by buses. Nicknamed 'The Route of the High and Mighty' it passed the Lord Provost's house and the homes of many councillors as it twisted its way through leafy south side suburbs. As a result, staff at Newlands tended to assign the best cars. Although scheduled to be one of the last routes, the Corporation bowed to pressure from British Railways that Maxwell Road railway bridge needed urgent renewal. As a result, the 3 became the last service along much of Sauchiehall Street, Renfield Street and over Glasgow Bridge.

Track abandoned: Park Road, Woodland Road, sections of Sauchiehall Street, part of Renfield Street, full length of service 3 west of Eglinton Toll and south from Albert Drive/Pollokshaws Road to Newlands depot. Union Street south to Albert Drive was retained to provide access to Coplawhill.

Last car: 1397 (Park Road-Mosspark-Newlands depot).

SERVICE PROFILE: 3

Above: **234, Woodlands Road, 8 July 1959.** This breakdown led to a major hold up with the defective car being eventually removed in the middle of a three-car 'tram train'. *David A. Brown*

Right: **Charing Cross.** An overview of the approach to this major junction. *G.W. Price collection*

1241, Sauchiehall Street, 1 April 1960. Severely damaged in the 1948 Newlands depot fire, this car lasted until June 1962. *John A. Clarke*

334, Renfield Street, May 1957. In its heyday, a car passed along this section every 12 seconds in each direction during peak hours. *Marcus Eavis/Online Transport Archive*

35, Jamaica Street, 2 July 1959. Standards last worked the 3 in early December 1959.
Hamish Stevenson/Online Transport Archive

1330, Eglinton Street, 4 June 1960. *E.C. Bennett & Martin Jenkins/Online Transport Archive*

Above left: 1393, Kenmure Street, 29 March 1960. The car is about to turn onto Albert Drive, one of eight right angle bends between Eglinton Toll and Mosspark. When lost in the Dalmarnock depot fire, this car had just had its ex-Liverpool trucks and motors replaced. *John A. Clarke*

Above right: Albert Drive, 4 June 1960. This car is taking up service from Newlands depot by using the single track connection from Pollokshaws Road which passed in front of Coplawhill works in order to reach Mosspark. On the left is the imposing Italian Renaissance style Albert Drive Church (1886/87) and in the distance the spire of Pollokshields Church of Scotland (1878) at the intersection with Shields Road. *E.C. Bennett & Martin Jenkins/Online Transport Archive*

Left: 466, Albert Drive, Pollokshields, 31 October 1958. *Hamish Stevenson/Online Transport Archive*

Below: 1325, St. Andrew's Drive/Nithsdale Road, 29 March 1960. *John A. Clarke*

532, Nithsdale Road, 10 May 1958. *Hamish Stevenson/Online Transport Archive*

538, Dumbreck Road, 29 May 1958. Until March 1959, any car bound for Newlands depot from any location displayed service number 8. The turreted baronial style Sherbrooke Castle hotel is still in business. *Hamish Stevenson/Online Transport Archive*

360, Mosspark Boulevard, September 1959. At one time, two morning specials from Newlands carried workers into the Govan area after which they reached Mosspark via Ibrox in order to transport businessmen into the city. *E.C. Bennett & Martin Jenkins/Online Transport Archive*

1148, Mosspark Boulevard, April 1959. *John Cadisch/Online Transport Archive*

Commensurate with closure of the 3, Newlands ceased to house trams. Once the city's largest depot, it had capacity for 201 cars on 20 tracks.

1298/1005, depot forecourt, 18 June 1949. In this early colour scene, each class of modern bogie double-decker is depicted including 1005. *Michael H. Waller/Online Transport Archive*

Depot overview, 6 April 1958. The stored Lightweight in the middle would be scrapped soon afterwards. *Paul de Beer/Online Transport Archive*

1397, Mosspark, 5 June 1960. The last service car to arrive at the depot. The following March, it was lost in the Dalmarnock depot fire. *E.C. Bennett & Martin Jenkins/ Online Transport Archive*

1395, depot entrance, 6 June 1960. This was the last car to leave the depot. All non-passenger movements such as this had a crew of two. 1395 was another Dalmarnock depot fire victim. *E.C. Bennett & Martin Jenkins/Online Transport Archive*

5 June 1960: Service 23 re-routed between New City Road and George Square by way of Cowcaddens, Hope Street and St Vincent Street. Cambridge Street plus part of Sauchiehall Street retained for an unspecified period for emergency use.

SECTION PROFILE: CAMBRIDGE STREET

53, Cambridge Street/Sauchiehall Street, 24 June 1958. *John A. Clarke*

1164, Cambridge Street/New City Road, 4 June 1960. *E.C. Bennett & Martin Jenkins// Online Transport Archive*

5 November 1960: service 23 (Maryhill to Baillieston – 9¾ miles, approx. 58 minutes) replaced by buses. Another well-used, long cross-city route requiring some 20 cars, it connected heavily-populated districts in the west and east ends before a semi-rural run to Baillieston. It was operated latterly from Dennistoun and Maryhill mostly by Coronations. **Track abandoned:** part of St Vincent Street, Queen Street, George Street, Duke Street and part of Shettleston Road). **Last cars:** 1262 (from Baillieston); 1223 (from Maryhill).

Maryhill Road, April 1959. Passing under the bridge carrying the Forth & Clyde Canal. *John Cadisch/Online Transport Archive*

1207, St George's Cross, 24 June 1958. Such was the volume of traffic using this busy five-way junction, it had to be completely relaid as late as October 1958. *John A. Clarke*

1205, St Vincent Street, 17 May 1959. This steeply-graded siding was used by cars from the east end short-working into the city. The points-cleaner is at the intersection with Hope Street and in the far distance a Standard turns from Renfield Street towards George Square. *G.W. Price collection*

George Square North, May 1957. *Marcus Eavis/Online Transport Archive*

1152, Duke Street, September 1958. *E.C. Bennett & Martin Jenkins/Online Transport Archive*

1238, Duke Street, Dennistoun, April 1959. Note the web of tram and trolleybus overhead wires. This Coronation was painted red when new in early 1939. *John Cadisch/ Online Transport Archive*

1201, Shettleston Road, September 1958. *E.C. Bennett & Martin Jenkins/Online Transport Archive*

1236, Shettleston Road/Westmuir Street (Shettleston Sheddings). The policeman on point duty is controlling traffic movements through the junction. *G.W. Price collection*

Baillieston Road, April 1959. This semi-rural section contrasted with the heavily-polluted industrial east end. *John Cadisch/Online Transport Archive*

1202/1045, Baillieston Road, Barachnie, 18 April 1959. In March 1961, 1202 was scorched in the Dalmarnock depot fire but returned to service for eight more months whilst 1045 lasted until October 1959. *Hamish Stevenson/Online Transport Archive*

Main Street, Baillieston, 1956. *Ray Bicknese/Online Transport Archive*

Main Street, Baillieston, September 1958. *E.C. Bennett & Martin Jenkins/Online Transport Archive*

Replacement of the 23 led to the complete closure of Dennistoun depot. Accessed by way of Paton Street, it could house 134 cars on seven tracks. Its trolleybuses went to Govan and its trams to Dalmarnock and Maryhill.

Above: 245, Paton Street, September 1958. *E.C. Bennett & Martin Jenkins/ Online Transport Archive*

Left: 1229, depot entrance, 5 November 1960. Some office staff pose with enthusiasts on the depot's final day. A few months later, this Coronation was consumed in the Dalmarnock conflagration. *David A. Brown*

Below: 1201, depot interior, October 1959. Trolleybuses had first arrived the previous year. *Garth Tilt*

6 November 1960: The 1¾ mile section of the 29 between Broomhouse and Tollcross closed without replacement. **Track abandoned:** Hamilton Road, part of Tollcross Road. **Last car:** 1359 (Broomhouse-Dalmarnock depot).

SECTION PROFILE: HAMILTON ROAD AND PART OF TOLLCROSS ROAD

36, Hamilton Road, 1956. The major traffic on this lightly-used section was to the zoo and a nearby crematorium. *Ray Bicknese/Online Transport Archive*

325, Hamilton Road, September 1958. *E.C. Bennett & Martin Jenkins/Online Transport Archive*

77, Hamilton Road, September 1958. The area around Mount Vernon railway bridge was semi-rural. *E.C. Bennett & Martin Jenkins/Online Transport Archive*

1013, Tollcross Road, September 1958. The crossover was located just outside the city boundary. Also discontinued were the Sunday afternoon specials between Anderston Cross and Broomhouse which showed the number 15. *E.C. Bennett & Martin Jenkins/Online Transport Archive*

1961

Now the last city system in the UK, Glasgow still had just under 40 miles of double-track worked by seven services from three depots by approximately 260 cars. A disastrous fire at Dalmarnock depot on 22 March 1961 destroyed 50 cars but extended the life of a handful of remaining Standards and Kilmarnock bogies. By 31 May 1961, the morning peak required 178 cars out of a total fleet of 190. 1089 last carried passengers on 2 June, the last Standard (1088) probably on 5 June, the last Kilmarnock sometime in August and 1100 on 1 November. During the year, trams disappeared from Springburn, Maryhill and the Royal Burgh of Rutherglen. Maryhill depot was also closed. Although maintenance levels were greatly reduced, up to three works cars would be out at night keeping the track and the surrounding setts in reasonable condition.

10 March 1961: Last shipyard specials between Whiteinch and Maryhill. **Track abandoned:** none. **Last car:** 1170 (from Whiteinch).

Above: **488, Scotstoun West, September 1958.** Maryhill-based 488 is outbound to Yoker ready to work a shipyard special. *E.C. Bennett & Martin Jenkins/Online Transport Archive*

Right: **97, Primrose Street, Whiteinch, June 1960.** *E.C. Bennett & Martin Jenkins/Online Transport Archive*

11 March 1961: Replacement of service 16 (Scotstoun-Keppochhill Road – 6 miles, 38 minutes). Worked latterly from Partick, this route skirted the central area, serving mostly densely-populated working class districts. **Track abandoned:** Hawthorn Street, Bilsland Drive, St George's Road, St Vincent Street (part). **Last cars:** 1176 (Keppochhill Road-Scotstoun-Partick depot); 1296 Scotstoun-Keppochhill Road-Partick depot).

GLASGOW
CORPORATION
TRAMWAYS
1 JANUARY 1961

Some peak hour services, shipyard
specials and other extras not shown

N
W E
S

Depots	
Dk	Dalmarnock
M	Maryhill
Pk	Partick
Other facilities	
CW	Coplawhill Works

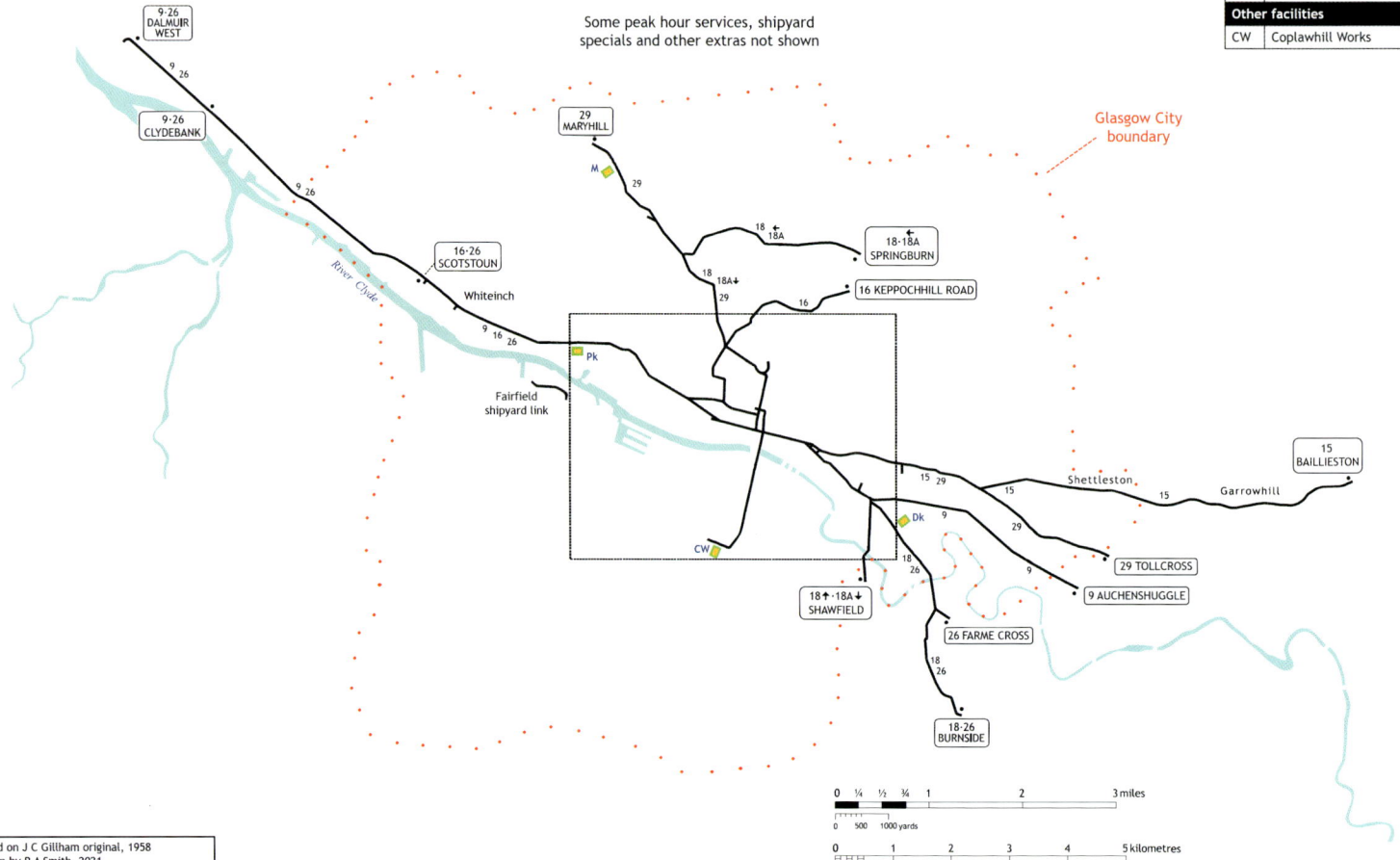

Glasgow City
boundary

9·26
DALMUIR
WEST

9 26

9·26
CLYDEBANK

9 26

16·26
SCOTSTOUN

9 26

Whiteinch

River Clyde

9 16 26

Pk

Fairfield
shipyard link

CW

29
MARYHILL

M

29

18
18A

18 18A

18·18A
SPRINGBURN

18A

29

16

16 KEPPOCHHILL ROAD

15
BAILLIESTON

Shettleston

Garrowhill

15 29

15

15

Dk

29

9

9

29 TOLLCROSS

9 AUCHENSHUGGLE

18
26

18·18A
SHAWFIELD

26 FARME CROSS

18
26

18·26
BURNSIDE

0 ¼ ½ ¾ 1 2 3 miles

0 500 1000 yards

0 1 2 3 4 5 kilometres

Based on J C Gillham original, 1958
Drawn by R A Smith, 2021
Adapted for this volume by Charles Roberts

1151/1312, Dalmuir, 30 March 1960. In peak hours, specials on the 16 headed west to the Clydebank industrial area. *John A. Clarke*

13, Scotstoun West, September 1958. A shipyard special is short-working to Possilpark. Note the entrance to Scotstoun West station and the two British Road Services Albion lorries. *E.C. Bennett & Martin Jenkins/Online Transport Archive*

1064/1119, Scotstoun, 24 March 1949. *Michael H. Waller/Online Transport Archive*

1300, Dumbarton Road, April 1958. A Cunarder heads towards the two railway bridges spanning the road on the approach to Partick. *John Cadisch/Online Transport Archive*

96, Dumbarton Road at Hayburn Street, Partick, 26 June 1958.

1249, St Vincent Street/Argyle Street, 1 April 1960.

29, St. George's Road, looking towards Woodlands Road, 7 July 1958.

1149, St George's Cross, 24 June 1958. Little of this once major five-way intersection remains today. *John A. Clarke (all)*

617, Round Toll, 24 June 1958. *John A. Clarke*

254, Keppochhill Road/Pinkston Road, 27 June 1958. *John A. Clarke*

1277, Keppochhill Road, March 1961. *Hamish Stevenson/Online Transport Archive*

376, Keppochhill Road, 1958. Note Sighthill cemetery on the right. *W.D. McMillan/ Travel Lens Photographic*

22 March 1961: At 12.53am, fire ripped through the southern section of Dalmarnock depot, destroying 50 trams in its wake, in a conflagration never fully explained. Management and Traffic officials, roused from their beds, ensured the depot's morning peak commitments were met by using spare cars from Maryhill and Partick depots as well as Coplawhill. During the ensuing days, the Works placed any serviceable tram back on the road including several awaiting scrap or set aside for preservation. However, the traffic situation remained tight until the conversion of service 10.

Lye 1 looking towards Lye 9. 1376, 1347, 108, 1387, 1157, 1337, 1354, 1316 and 1202. This view taken hours after the fire had been brought under control. *G.W. Price collection*

1376, 1347 and 108; lyes 1-3, 22 March 1961. *Hamish Stevenson/Online Transport Archive*

Lyes 8-9 partially cleared, March 1961. *W. Fisher*

108 and 1387; lyes 3 and 4. Cars buried under tangled steelwork. *Harry Luff collection/ Online Transport Archive*

1157, 1337, and 1354; lyes 5, 6 and 7. These mangled remains had also been damaged by collapsing cleaning galleries. *Brian Longworth/Online Transport Archive*

Albert Drive. This unidentified Cunarder has been towed to Coplawhill for scrap.

Ian Stewart/Online Transport Archive

Lyes 5-9. By April 12 these had been cleared and traction poles planted.

G. W. Price collection

3 June 1961: Operated from Dalmarnock and Maryhill depots, former white service 18 (Springburn–Burnside, 8¾ miles, 56 minutes) and service 18A (Springburn–Shawfield, 7 miles, 46 minutes) were replaced by buses. Cars returning from Shawfield showed 18. These cross-city services required a maximum of 34 cars and were the last to serve industrial Springburn and residential Burnside. As a result, buses appeared on the city centre section of Argyle Street for the first time. **Track abandoned:** Hawthorn Street, Bilsland Drive, St George's Road, Sauchiehall Street, Elmbank Street, Bothwell Street, Main Street, Bridgeton, Rutherglen Bridge and Glasgow Road to Shawfield Stadium; also Farmeloan Road, Stonelaw Road and Dukes Road. **Last cars:** Either 1195 or 1196 (from Shawfield), 1190 (Burnside-Springburn-Maryhill depot); 488 (Springburn-Burnside-Dalmarnock depot).

SERVICE PROFILE: 18, 18A

488, Springburn terminus, 3 June 1961. Restored for a Paris museum, it returned to service after the fire. This area is virtually unrecognisable today. *Martin Jenkins/ Online Transport Archive*

1277/466, Hawthorn Street, 27 June 1958. Outside Possilpark depot. *John A. Clarke*

Junction of Bilsland Drive and Hawthorn Street. Note the landmark Water Tower at Ruchill Hospital. The site has been cleared but the tower remains. *Garth Tilt*

1367, Bilsland Drive, 31 March 1960. West of the Forth & Clyde Canal aqueduct. *John A. Clarke*

1204, Maryhill Road/Vernon Street. The Coronation has derailed on the crossover causing disruption. *Roy Hamilton*

St. George's Road/Woodlands Road, early June 1961. *E.C. Bennett & Martin Jenkins/ Online Transport Archive*

Above: 1201, Sauchiehall Street/Elmbank Street, early June 1961. Note the classic Art Deco Beresford Hotel built in 1938. *E.C. Bennett & Martin Jenkins/Online Transport Archive*

Right: 77, St Vincent Street/Elmbank Street. The car is returning to Maryhill depot. *Hamish Stevenson/Online Transport Archive*

Below left: 1346, Bothwell Street, June 1961. Cars from both directions short-worked to here. On this occasion, a damaged Cunarder is causing a major hold-up. *Hamish Stevenson/Online Transport Archive*

Below right: 1212, Bothwell Street/Hope Street, 2 June 1961. As soon as the last 18s had passed, the crew of works car 40 removed the electric point equipment. *E.C. Bennett & Martin Jenkins/Online Transport Archive*

169, Trongate, 1960. This car was working a special bound for Ruchill Hospital.
Ian Stewart/Online Transport Archive

1187, London Road, 1961. 'The Barras', Glasgow's famous market and entertainment centre was a popular attraction at weekends. *Ian Stewart/Online Transport Archive*

Bridgeton Cross, pre-1957. Note the ornate cast iron shelter and clock tower. In front of it is the tramway cabin cabin from where movements through this complex junction were controlled. *G.W. Price collection*

Bridgeton Cross, September 1959. From here, the 18 proceeded to Burnside via Dalmarnock Road, the 18A to Shawfield via Main Street. *E.C. Bennett & Martin Jenkins/Online Transport Archive*

Main Street, Bridgeton, 3 June 1961. A typical Glasgow 'canyon', very much a feature of the city suburbs. *Martin Jenkins/Online Transport Archive*

1373, Rutherglen Bridge. This was one of three east end bridges used by trams to cross the Clyde. Note the old gas lamp still in place. *Hamish Stevenson/Online Transport Archive*

Glasgow Road/Shawfield Drive. On arrival at Shawfield, conductors changed the service number to 18 for the return to Springburn. *E.C. Bennett & Martin Jenkins/Online Transport Archive*

1313, Glasgow Road/Rutherglen Road, 3 June 1961. For many years, Shawfield was served by 'Dog Track specials' catering for the nearby Greyhound Stadium. This was the very last one to operate. *The Transport Library*

1328, Ruby Street. This car is taking up service from Dalmarnock depot and will turn onto Dalmarnock Road used by services 18 and 26 to Burnside. *Tony Belton*

Dalmarnock Bridge, early June 1961. Note the cast-iron boundary marker. This was the last bridge to carry service trams over the Clyde. *E.C. Bennett & Martin Jenkins/ Online Transport Archive*

1194, Farmeloan Road, 1 June 1961. *Ian L. Cormack/Online Transport Archive*

1324, Stonelaw Road/Rutherglen Main Street. *Hamish Stevenson/Online Transport Archive*

3 June 1961: Service 26 (Scotstoun or Clydebank-Burnside, 8¼ miles, 53 minutes and 10½ miles, 60 minutes, respectively) cut back from Burnside to Farme Cross. **Last car:** 1203 (Burnside-Dalmarnock depot).

SECTION PROFILE: FARMELOAN ROAD-BURNSIDE

1317/1279, Stonelaw Road, Rutherglen. 1279 was blitzed, burned twice and rebodied twice. *Hamish Stevenson/Online Transport Archive*

1174, Stonelaw Road/Johnstone Drive, early June 1961. The track on this section was in good condition. *E.C. Bennett & Martin Jenkins/Online Transport Archive*

Above: **Stonelaw Woods, May 1957.** *John Cadisch/Online Transport Archive*

Right: **1098, Duke's Road, Burnside, 1948.** *R.R. Clark/Scottish Tramway & Transport Society*

21 October 1961: Worked from Dalmarnock and Maryhill depots, former green car service 29, (Maryhill-Tollcross, 8 miles, 48 minutes) replaced by buses. Interestingly, cars from the Maryhill direction running into Dalmarnock depot showed 26. Requiring some 36 cars, the frequent well-patronised cross-city 29 catered for densely populated older neighbourhoods as well quieter outer suburban areas. **Track abandoned:** Maryhill Road, Gairbraid Avenue stub, New City Road, Cowcaddens Street, Maitland Street stub, Hope Street (above St Vincent Street), Rowchester Street, Tollcross Road. **Last cars:** 1215 (Tollcross-Dalmarnock depot); 1279 (Glasgow Cross-Maryhill depot; owing to the driver being inebriated, an inspector took over at Normal School and instead of going to Maryhill terminus the journey was terminated at Maryhill depot which now closed to trams.)

SERVICE PROFILE: 29

Maryhill depot, April 1958. Accommodating 93 trams on 21 tracks, this was one of two depots with an allocation of ex-Liverpool cars. At the end it still had some 25 cars including one-off 1005, which was transferred to Partick. *Paul de Beer/ Online Transport Archive*

556, Maryhill terminus. An unusual view of this location in the snow. *Photographer unknown/Travel Lens Photographic*

522, Gairbraid Avenue siding. The conductress is resetting the destination screen for the next trip. Latterly, a few cars departed from here during the weekday evening peak. It was also used to short-turn late running cars. *Garth Tilt*

1340/1238/1147/1036, Maryhill Road/Kelvinside Avenue, 31 March 1960. Cars delayed by a traction pole replacement. Note the Overhead Line Department's 1939 Albion lorry. *John A. Clarke*

582, Maryhill Road/Queen's Cross. *G.W. Price collection*

1378, St George's Cross, 14 October 1961. The Cunarder is turning from Maryhill Road into New City Road. *Hamish Stevenson/Online Transport Archive*

1241, New City Road/Cambridge Street, October 1961. Note the overhead has been removed from the latter. *Hamish Stevenson/Online Transport Archive*

1148, Cowcaddens Street, 4 August 1960. At peak times, cars used a number of short-turn points in the central area including this one. However, on this occasion, the car is trapped in a tram-jam. *R.B. Parr/Scottish Tramway & Transport Society*

1015/1359, Hope Street. Parallel parking at its best! 1359 would be re-railed when road traffic permitted. The priority was to keep the services running. *John A.N. Emslie*

1286, Argyle Street/Queen Street, 1961. A typically busy Saturday scene with hundreds of shoppers out and about. *Ian Stewart/Online Transport Archive*

77, Moir Street. Many peak hour extras departed from here providing additional capacity between Glasgow Cross and Maryhill. *Garth Tilt*

1171, Gallowgate near Abercromby Street, June 1961. *E.C. Bennett & Martin Jenkins/Online Transport Archive*

Gallowgate/Croft Street, October 1961. Note the former LMS railway bridge in the background. *E.C. Bennett & Martin Jenkins/Online Transport Archive*

156/506, Gallowgate at Parkhead. The Round dash Standard passes on a short working towards the city. *Hamish Stevenson/Online Transport Archive*

Tollcross Road, October 1961. The entrance to Parkhead depot is in the background on the right. *E.C. Bennett & Martin Jenkins/Online Transport Archive*

Tollcross Road, October 1961. A Central SMT Lodekka bus and Coronation tram pass by well-preserved tenements which still stand today. *E.C. Bennett & Martin Jenkins/ Online Transport Archive*

Tollcross Road/Braidfauld Street, 21 October 1961. *G.W. Price/Online Transport Archive*

1348, Tollcross, June 1961. Three cars wait their turn to reverse. *Martin Jenkins/Online Transport Archive*

22 October 1961: On Sunday morning, trams at Maryhill depot were sent in groups for relocation to Dalmarnock or Partick. Those destined for Partick were scheduled to use the Queen Street crossover on Argyle Street in order to reverse. However, roadworks prevented this so the convoy had to return to Maryhill until later in the day when the path to Partick was clear!

Right: Last to leave, 1222, even visited Maryhill terminus before setting off for Partick. This view shows transferring cars queueing up to reverse in Argyle Street in order to reach Partick depot. *Alex Brown/Travel Lens Photographic*

22 October 1961: Service 26 (Scotstoun-Farme Cross) cut back to Dalmarnock. **Track abandoned:** Cambuslang Road, part of Dalmarnock Road. **Last car:** 1224 (Farme Cross-Dalmarnock depot).

SECTION PROFILE: FARME CROSS-DALMARNOCK

1306/1307, Farme Cross, 29 March 1960. This was the last route carrying passengers across the Clyde. *John A. Clarke*

1134, Dalmarnock Road, 18 May 1959. The car is heading towards Dalmarnock power station (visible in background). *G.W. Price collection*

1962

A landmark year in the annals of Glasgow Corporation Transport. Tramway conversion on schedule for completion by September. To work the remaining 22 miles there was an active fleet of just under 100 cars consisting of a 1005 and ever-grubbier Coronations and Cunarders. Spiralling traffic congestion and staff retention amongst the biggest problems in the department's drive for economy.

Mid-January: Officials working over arrangements for the final procession.

10 March 1962: Former green service 15 (Anderston Cross-Baillieston, 6¾ miles, 37 minutes) replaced by buses. Operated from Dalmarnock (and formerly Dennistoun and Parkhead depots), this heavy line required a maximum turn-out of 25 cars. The last of the few routes to terminate in the central area, it served commercial, industrial, residential and rural areas including nearly two miles outside the city boundary. **Track abandoned:** Gallowgate east from Moir Street, Westmuir Street, Shettleston Road and Baillieston Road. Depot only track on Springfield Road also closed. **Last car:** 1242 (Anderston Cross-Baillieston-Dalmarnock Depot. Departure from Baillieston delayed by 10 minutes. Power had been switched off as the tram entered Shettleston. Restored after ten minutes. Sub-station staff had assumed tram already in the depot! Very fast run to Dalmarnock. Arrived 20 minutes late.)

SERVICE PROFILE: 15

1360, Anderston Cross. This area subsequently wiped out by motorway construction.
G.W. Price collection

Argyle Street. Looking towards Anderston Cross. The car is approaching the crossover at Douglas Street. Another scene with many background changes.
G.W. Price collection

Hope Street, 29 March 1960. As the result of a fire at a whisky warehouse, part of Argyle Street was closed from 28 March to 1 April 1960 leading to service 15 being diverted via Hope Street to terminate in St Vincent Street. *Hamish Stevenson/Online Transport Archive*

1045, Argyle Street/Buchanan Street, 1955. *W.J. Wyse/LRTA (London Area)/Online Transport Archive*

1141/1330, Glasgow Cross, June 1961. This major junction at the east end of Trongate was also a reversing point for trams short-working from the east on service 15. *E.C. Bennett & Martin Jenkins/Online Transport Archive*

1247, Gallowgate/Market Street, 2 June 1961. This was another of the city's famous densely-populated tenement-lined streets. Much of this area has since been redeveloped. *E.C. Bennett & Martin Jenkins/Online Transport Archive*

1231, Rowchester Street, Whitevale. This siding off Gallowgate continued to be used as an evening peak hour loading point probably until early 1961. Whitevale depot which closed in 1922 is visible in the background. *Hamish Stevenson/Online Transport Archive*

370, Shettleston Sheddings, junction of Shettleston Road and Westmuir Street, April 1960. Working a Special, inbound from Garrowhill to Whitevale. *John A. Clarke*

1148/1217, Shettleston Road/McNair Street. This crossover was used regularly during peak periods by cars short-working to Shettleston which made their way back to the city or Dalmarnock depot. *Hamish Stevenson/Online Transport Archive*

Baillieston Road/Sandyhills. This location is east of the Glasgow City Boundary.
Hamish Stevenson/Online Transport Archive

1233, Baillieston Road/Sandyhills, 1956. Today, houses have spread over both sides of this one-time rural road. Note the contrast between the stooks of corn and the new housing. *Ray Bicknese/Online Transport Archive*

12, Baillieston Road/Carrick Drive, Autumn 1960. The Overhead line department are in attendance as the driver edges cautiously under a wire that has become detached from the span wire. *Brian Longworth/Online Transport Archive*

Above: **1045, Garrowhill, April 1959.** A trio of Goddesses congregate at this part-way crossover which was well-used at peak times. *E.C. Bennett & Martin Jenkins/Online Transport Archive*

Left: **Baillieston Road, Barrachnie, 10 March 1962.** On the final day, an unidentified Cunarder accelerates rapidly downhill towards Sandyhills and Shettleston. *G.W. Price/Online Transport Archive*

1322, Baillieston Main Street/ Maxwell Street. *Hamish Stevenson/Online Transport Archive*

Baillieston Main Street/Church Street. Note the outline of the track which once led into the nearby sub-station. *G.W. Price/Online Transport Archive*

1238, Baillieston Main Street. This was then a bustling commercial street with a variety of local shops. *Hamish Stevenson/Online Transport Archive*

1172, Baillieston, 1958. Until November 1956, trams had continued to Coatbridge and Airdrie. *M.J. Lea/LRTA (London Area)/Online Transport Archive*

18 March 1962: Moir Street loop discontinued but stub retained off London Road for short-working trams. **Track abandoned:** Gallowgate (Moir Street-Trongate).

2 June 1962: Former red/green service 26 (Clydebank or Scotstoun to Dalmarnock, 9 miles, 57 minutes and 6¾ miles, 43 minutes respectively) replaced by buses. Operated from Partick and Dalmarnock depots, this busy route served Clydeside industry, shipyards, commercial and residential districts. **Track abandoned:** Dalmarnock Road (from Ruby Street to just north of Dalmarnock Bridge), Hayburn Street. **Last cars:** 1318 (Scotstoun-Dalmarnock-Dalmarnock depot), 1263 (Yoker-Partick depot), 1261 (Scotstoun-Partick depot), 1270 (last car into Partick depot off service 9). Latterly housing around 30 cars, Partick depot closed to trams and 1005, together with withdrawn single-decker 1089, were transferred for storage at Coplawhill

▮ SERVICE PROFILE: 26

1398, Clydebank, 2 June 1962. Clydebank Town Hall is visible in background. *Martin Jenkins/Online Transport Archive*

1186, Dumbarton Road, 30 March 1960. Extra shipyard specials were needed to handle the crowds at finishing time at John Brown's shipyard at Clydebank. *John A. Clarke*

Above: 1232, Balmoral Street, Scotstoun, 1962. For many years, this had been the stub terminus for services 6, 16 and 26. Albion Motors' commercial vehicle plant was located beyond the bridge. *Tony Belton*

Right: 1102, Dumbarton Road. Approaching Whiteinch, the car is about to pass the local Odeon cinema and a tradesman's horse and cart. *Hamish Stevenson/Online Transport Archive*

Below left: 1301, Dumbarton Road/Hayburn Street. This view of the junction with the approach road to Partick depot was taken from Partick Hill Station. *Hamish Stevenson/Online Transport Archive*

Below right: 1151, Dumbarton Road/Merkland Street. *Hamish Stevenson/ Online Transport Archive*

35, Argyle Street, approaching Kelvingrove Art Gallery and Museum, September 1959. The former Western Infirmary can be seen in the background. *Ian Stewart/Online Transport Archive*

766, Argyle Street. This view taken between St Vincent Street and Anderston Cross shows the granite slab wagon way which made life easier for horses pulling heavy loads uphill from docklands. *R.J.S. Wiseman/National Tramway Museum*

1099, Argyle Street/Union Street. Note the Seddon lorry with its sheeted load creeping up on the nearside. *Ian Stewart/Online Transport Archive*

1361, Trongate. The Cunarder is held up by a tram-jam. *F.E.J. Ward/Online Transport Archive*

1340, London Road/Moir Street. This disabled car was being towed into the siding under supervision of a GCT traffic inspector. Prompt action like this kept trams moving on the London Road corridor. *Hamish Stevenson/Online Transport Archive*

London Road, May 1962. Note the sharp reverse curves located near 'The Barras'. *G.W. Price/Online Transport Archive*

1284, Bridgeton Cross, August 1962 All property survives, albeit the shops have changed. *Tony Belton*

1315/1359, Dalmarnock Road, August 1962. The cars are passing near the former LMS railway bridge. *Tony Belton*

Dalmarnock Road/Springfield Road, 2 June 1962. The tracks into the latter have been recently lifted. Also on view is Central SMT Leyland PD2 L405. *Martin Jenkins/Online Transport Archive*

1318, Dalmarnock, 2 June 1962. The last car from the terminus was photographed prior to making the half-mile run to Dalmarnock Depot. *G.W. Price/Online Transport Archive*

1270, Hayburn Street, 2 June 1962. The very last tram to enter Partick depot was preceded by a Piper accompanied by a procession of local residents. *Martin Jenkins/Online Transport Archive*

Partick depot (capacity 124 cars on 21 tracks). Admin offices to the left and the glazed staff notice boards centre. *Ian Stewart/Online Transport Archive*

3 June 1962: Early morning departures on service 9 from Dalmuir West and late evening journeys from Queen Street to Scotstoun, Yoker and Dalmuir West worked mainly by buses.

26 August 1962: Last Sunday specials operated on service 9.

31 August 1962: Last weekday specials operated on service 9.

1 September 1962: Former red service 9 (Auchenshuggle-Dalmuir West, 12 miles, 69 minutes) replaced by buses. This was the final day of the UK's last classic city tram route. Worked from Dalmarnock and Partick (until June 1962) depots, it was one of the heaviest lines serving the city centre, commercial, industrial and residential areas as well as townships along the north bank of the Clyde. At peak times, the regular service was supplemented by additional shipyard specials and intermediate short workings. On this final day, 40 out of the 62 cars at Dalmarnock were in use together with three cars on private hires. **Track abandoned:** None. **Last cars:** 1198 (Dalmuir West-Auchenshuggle-Dalmarnock depot); 1383 (Auchenshuggle-Dalmuir West-Dalmarnock depot); 1313 (Auchenshuggle-Yoker-Dalmarnock depot).

SERVICE PROFILE: 9

1249, Dalmuir, summer 1962. Central SMT Leyland PD2 L585 has crashed through a wall and bent a tram standard, separating the span wire from the trolley wire forcing the driver of the Coronation to pass with caution. *Tony Belton*

Forth & Clyde Canal swing bridge, Dalmuir, 18 August 1962. A perfect reflection. The opening and closing of the bridge was controlled from the cabin to the left of the tram.
David F. Russell

Dumbarton Road, 1 September 1962. Shipyard cranes provide a backdrop for this Coronation tram passing through Clydebank. *G.W. Price/Online Transport Archive*

142, Dumbarton Road/Kilbowie Road, 24 March 1949. This Standard had been experimentally converted into a bogie car and was active from December 1947 to March 1954. The crew off a Duntocher tram can be seen heading for their meal break at a local bothy or café. *Michael H. Waller/Online Transport Archive*

1383, Dumbarton Road/Clydebank. A John Brown's shipyard 0-4-0 Saddle Tank causes a slight delay as it crosses the main road under supervision. *G.W. Price collection*

1176, Dumbarton Road/Mill Road, Yoker, 18 August 1962. Note the splendid enamel British Railways sign pointing towards Yoker High Station. *David F. Russell*

1175, Dumbarton Road/Kingsway, 1962. A typical weekday evening rush-hour with buses and trams dominating this scene at Scotstoun West. *Ian Stewart/Online Transport Archive*

1111, Dumbarton Road. Workmen attend to a fishplate joint between Scotstoun and Whiteinch. *W.D. McMillan/Travel Lens Photographic*

1310, Dumbarton Road/Sandiman Street. The car is passing well-known local Balshagray School. A similarly designed school building existed on London Road in front of Celtic Park. *Hamish Stevenson/Online Transport Archive*

Dumbarton Road/Hayburn Street, 2 June 1961. The Cunarder is about to run off service into Partick depot as a Blue Train multiple unit, introduced 1960 for the electrification of the Glasgow suburban railway network, passes overhead. *Martin Jenkins/Online Transport Archive*

1202, Dumbarton Road, 2 June 1961. A splendid view of Partick looking west along Dumbarton Road towards Partick Hill station in the distance. *Martin Jenkins/ Online Transport Archive*

1272, Argyle Street/Finnieston Street, 2 June 1961. Finnieston loop was used as the starting point for a number of westbound peak hour specials as well as by cars from the west terminating here and returning to Partick depot. *E.C. Bennett & Martin Jenkins/ Online Transport Archive*

1091, Argyle Street, August 1956. The car is emerging from the Heilandman's Umbrella on a rain-soaked Saturday afternoon with shoppers scurrying to keep dry. *R.J.S. Wiseman/National Tramway Museum*

London Road/Glasgow Cross. A Coronation passes under the railway bridge as a steam-hauled passenger train crosses above having just left St Enoch's Station (closed 1966). *A.S. Clayton/Online Transport Archive*

1148, London Road/ Bridgeton Cross, 19 May 1962. This was the last place in the UK where trams and trolleybuses shared the same road. TB54, a 1958 BUT with Crossley body, glides past on service 106 for Millerston. *G.W. Price/Online Transport Archive*

1115, London Road, June 1960. Withdrawn after thirty-two years' service in 1961, the car is now at the National Tramway Museum. Here, it passes Celtic Park. *E.C. Bennett & Martin Jenkins/Online Transport Archive*

1319, London Road/Belvidere Hospital, 3 June 1962. The floodlights of Celtic FC can be seen in the background. *G.W. Price/Online Transport Archive*

London Road/St Peter's Cemetery, 3 June 1962. Passengers alight to pay their respects to lost loved ones. *G.W. Price/Online Transport Archive*

341, London Road, 22 March 1949. This is the original Auchenshuggle terminus near Braidfauld Street. *Michael H. Waller/Online Transport Archive*

1233, London Road, 1962. The car is approaching the later Auchenshuggle terminus with the Clyde Ironworks railway embankment in the background. *Ted Relton/Online Transport Archive*

1154/1383, Dalmuir West, 1 September 1962. Cars prepare to make the final public departures. *Hamish Stevenson/Online Transport Archive*

1313, Dalmarnock Road/Ruby Street, 2 September 1962. The last tram from Yoker arrived 20 minutes late in the early hours of Sunday morning. Headboard drawn by author Geoff Price and fixed by Mike Mercer. *J.L. Stevenson*

2-4 September 1962: Special part day service operated between Anderston Cross and Auchenshuggle at a flat fare of 6d with special pink souvenir tickets. End of special service. **Track abandoned:** Stobcross Street, Moir Street, London Road (Bridgeton Cross-Auchenshuggle) and Abercromby Street.

1219, Moir Street, 2 September 1962. 1181 became defective and was pushed onto Moir Street siding by 1219. Both cars overshot the overhead wire and were eventually retrieved by 1174. The service was erratic for a few hours. *Tony Belton*

1243, London Road/Davaar Street, 2 September 1962. LA13 was one of the striking fleet of replacement Leyland Atlantean buses. *Tony Belton*

1360, London Road/Charlotte Street, 4 September 1962. After enthusiasts had badgered depot staff to roster a Cunarder for the final day of the special service, two appeared. *Tony Belton*

1174, Ruby Street, 4 September 1962. Scotland's last public service tramcar returns to the depot for the final time at 5.50pm as crowds gather for the final procession. *Tony Belton*

4 September 1962: Last Tram Procession. Over 250,000 people turned out, despite heavy rain, to line the 3¾ mile route to bid a final farewell to their much loved trams. Some of the 20 vehicles were reserved for invited guests whilst others carried members of the public. Special green souvenir tickets were issued. The procession started at 6.30pm.

534, Bridgeton Cross/London Road. This restored horse car was at the head of the procession of twenty trams which included superbly restored historic cars followed by a mix of washed and cleaned Coronations and Cunarders. *Nigel McMillan/Online Transport Archive*

779, London Road. Large crowds watched the procession slowly move past Barrowland towards the city centre. 779 was dedicated to the HLI Battallion raised by the transport department in 1914. *Hamish Stevenson/Online Transport Archive*

672, Bridge Street. This 'Room and Kitchen' car of 1898 was driven by Motorman William Trotter. Also on board where Lord Provost, Jean Roberts and General Manager, Eric Fitzpayne. *Martin Jenkins/Online Transport Archive*

1363, Albert Drive. In torrential rain, after passengers on the public cars alighted on Pollokshaws Road, pennies were placed on the rails here for a final souvenir. Within minutes of the last tram moving into the works, the street was deserted. *Hamish Stevenson/Online Transport Archive*

6 September 1962: Not to be outdone, the Burgh of Clydebank chartered their own 'Last Tram' for a final, final run! Staffed by William Trotter and Conductress Elsie Sulter, 1282 collected the Official Party from Clydebank Town Hall. Also on board were Manager Fitzpayne, his son Alan and Chief Inspector Priestman. **Track abandoned:** everything west of the Hope Street/Argyle Street junction. **Last car:** 1282. A long-standing rumour suggesting Works Car 40 made a complete round trip on 8 September 1962, between Auchenshuggle and Dalmuir West, dropping off equipment for track-lifting gangs, has never been confirmed.

Dumbarton Road/Merkland Street. The 'last Clydebank' was shadowed throughout by mobile Inspectors, who had earlier checked that the tracks were still usable at a point where a new zebra crossing was being installed at Merkland Street, Partick. *Hamish Stevenson/Online Transport Archive*

Dumbarton Road, Clydebank. Watched by interested onlookers, the car awaits the Official Party outside the Town Hall for their ceremonial final tram ride through the Burgh. 1282 departed 7.13pm. *Nigel McMillan*

Dalmuir West. Significant numbers of local people were on hand to see the car leave for Yoker. *Garth Tilt*

Yoker. Having crossed the Burgh boundary, 1282 reversed and returned to the Town Hall. After reversing again, it made the lone 10 mile trip back to Dalmarnock depot with young Alan Fitzpayne at the controls for much of the way. On Dalmarnock Road, STMS/STTS member Willie Guthrie hailed the car which stopped. On boarding, Willie became the last ever fare paying passenger when he was issued with a ticket by conductress Elsie Sulter. *Garth Tilt*

A reminder of Dalmarnock depot (capacity 119 cars on 25 tracks).

1374 and others, lyes 1 and 2. These cars were waiting removal to Coplawhill for dismantling. *Nigel McMillan*

1154, 1 April 1960. The only recognisable feature today is the sub-station (left) surrounded by low rise housing. *John A. Clarke*

Above: **Interior view, 31 August 1962.** Note the painter refreshing the lye numbers in readiness for the Last Tram procession. Invited guests boarded their trams in the covered section of the depot. *G.W. Price collection*

Left: **Lyes 1-4.** An AEC Matador was used to shunt defective trams onto these unwired lyes. *Hamish Stevenson/ Online Transport Archive*

15 September 1962. Track abandoned: All remaining track between Dalmarnock depot and Pollokshaws Road/Albert Drive.

With its varied fleet of works cars, other miscellaneous rolling stock, piles of new and used rails and stacks of lamps and sleepers, Barrland Street Permanent Way yard was a real Aladdin's cave for enthusiasts.

Barrland Street. Staff assemble trackwork prior to its installation somewhere on the network. *G.W. Price collection*

No. 32, April 1958. Formerly Paisley District 1002, this car is coupled to its designated crane-mounted trailer. *Paul de Beer/Online Transport Archive*

1100, 2 September 1962. Touring the remaining trackage, the last privately hired tram also circumnavigated Barrland Street yard. *Tony Belton*

1190, Barrland Street. Post closure, cars awaiting scrap were stored here and inside the works. *Hamish Stevenson/Online Transport Archive*

This remarkable photographic journey ends, appropriately, at Coplawhill carworks (1899) where so many trams were built, rebuilt, renovated, repaired, painted and scrapped. Occupying 23,000 square yards, the works employed 1,200 people at its peak. Every tram underwent a five year annual overhaul programme, the whole process taking three weeks. Also on site was the Motor School which contained a skeleton tram body and a bank of tramcar controllers for trainees to learn how a tramcar worked.

13 February 1963: 1245 pushed 1274 into position for preservation collection. Power switched off. **Track abandoned:** Albert Drive.

15 April 1964: former Paint Shop section reopened as the Museum of Transport.

Above left: **Cars being restored, early 1962.** Some of the workforce are engaged restoring trams destined for preservation. Today, Glasgow trams can still be seen at the city's Riverside Museum, Summerlee Industrial Heritage Museum, the National Tramway Museum, East Anglia Transport Museum and the Seashore Trolley Museum, USA. *Martin Jenkins/Online Transport Archive*

Above right: **New Cunarders, early 1950.** The works was always a hive of activity. *A.D. Packer*

Left: **No. 3, April 1958.** The wheel comes full circle. The oldest surviving electric tram dating from 1898 was renumbered 3 when it was converted into a Mains Testing Car. It is pictured in the main avenue of the works prior to its restoration and participation in the final procession as 672. It was subsequently displayed in the city's first Museum of Transport. *Paul de Beer/Online Transport Archive*